Return To
GETHSEMANE

John O'Brien OFM

First Published in Great Britain by
Pen Press Publishers Ltd
39-41 North Road
London N7 9DP

ISBN 1 900796 88 0

Cover design by Catrina Sherlock
'Crows over the wheat field' by Vincent Van Gogh
Vincent Van Gogh Foundation, Amsterdam

Return To GETHSEMANE

John O'Brien OFM

Pen Press Publishers Ltd
London

DEDICATION

For my late mother Joan,
and for my father, Patrick, sisters Kirry and Annette and
brother-in-law Michael and for the new generation of Coley,
Nigel and Michaela.

About the Author

The author joined the Franciscan Order in 1975 and studied Philosophy and Theology. He has been an ordained priest since 1985 and has worked as a teacher, chaplain and advisor in Ireland where he lives.

ACKNOWLEDGEMENTS

There is a large number of people who helped me in my work. The first person I would like to thank is Dr. Vincent Molony who encouraged me to start writing again. I would like to thank others who encouraged and helped me, especially Mike Ganly, Frank and Emily Young, Sr Brid Geraghty and the Sisters of The Divine Master (Athlone), Shaun Edwards, O.B.E., Noel and Anne McKervey, Tara Owens, Sean McGorisk, Aidan and May Kelly.

Teresa Hand Campbell helped with the typing and helped me get organised (no mean achievement). Sheona Burke, Olga Corrigan and Cora Quinn also helped with the typing. Olga Corrigan and Br. Pio Rizzo (St Pauls Book Centre, Athlone) and Cathedral Bookshop (Dublin) were very helpful to me in tracking down books.

Other groups in Athlone helped. They include, T.S.B., Bank of Ireland, The Irish Permanent, First Active, N.I.B. and Elan Pharmaceuticals.

I would like to thank all at Pen Press, Grace, Lynn, Catrina, Lisa and Linda who provided much needed support and encouragement. Last but not least I would like to thank Angela Blacoe, Joe Lalor, Sean Murphy, O.F.M. and Eammon O'Driscoll O.F.M for their support.

John O'Brien,
The Friary,
Athlone.
2000

Also by the author
Catch The Wind   ISBN 1 900796 10 4   £6.95
Pray Through Depression   ISBN 1 900796 31 7   £3.95
Published by Pen Press Publishers Ltd

CONTENTS

CHAPTER 1

THERE IS NO NEED TO STAY THERE

'Lord my God, I call for help by day;
I cry at night before you.
Let my prayer come into your presence.
O turn your ear to my cry.

For my soul is filled with evils;
my life is on the brink of the grave,
I am reckoned as one in the tomb:
I have reached the end of my strength,
Lord, why do you reject me?
Why do you hide your face?

Wretched, close to death from my youth,
I have borne your trials; I am numb.
Your fury has swept down upon me;
your terrors have utterly destroyed me.

They surround me all the day like a flood,
they assail me all together.
Friend and a neighbour you have taken away:
my one companion is darkness.' (Ps 88)

Psalm 88 is associated with the site in Jerusalem, St. Peter in Gallicantu, where Jesus is believed to have been imprisoned the night before his death. This psalm is put on the lips of Jesus. It would have been the psalm his people would have used in desolation. It expresses his loneliness and anguish as he is rejected by almost all and faces the prospect of a violent death. It helps express the profound

1

anguish that many people go through. The line 'my one companion is darkness' is a line that speaks to me. At one occasion in my life I became ill, both mentally and physically. During this time I experienced many traumatic experiences, which drove me further into depression. The words of the psalm hit home. My faith in humankind had all but disintegrated and my faith in God was battered. I tried to pray but at that time God appeared silent.

'Illness' can be used as a much wider term than 'disease'.[1] It can embrace my response, and that of my social environment, to a disease: For instance I can feel lonely and isolated. In the Bible the symptoms of a disease are very rarely mentioned. It is rather the total situation of the sufferer, his relationship with God and his fellow human beings that occupies the centre of attention. The details of the symptoms of the disease are left tantalizingly vague.

It is in this sense of the term that Ps 88 speaks and which I use when I speak of my 'illness'. I refer to my situation in myself as I found myself caught in the world of darkness. The causes of the depression are not mentioned in order that I may use the more general term, illness. In this way I share my experience with those who find themselves in the same predicament. Many different events bring people to this point. Depression as illness can arise from many different sources - rejection, bereavement, burn-out, traumatic experiences such as abuse of any kind - sexual, emotional, physical - or as a reaction to a protracted illness.

My aim in this work is to share with you, the reader, the journey I am undertaking in my healing. In this way I pray that those who suffer illness and depression may realise they are not alone and that they may be able to come to healing in their lives, or at least have the courage to begin. I am not writing as one who is totally healed. I am still in the process of being healed. There are still times when I feel that my one companion is darkness and I have to start again.

The Illness of Depression

It is difficult to put into words how depression strikes and how, when it does, one perceives God and fellow human beings. I found mood songs by bands like The Rolling Stones and The Doors helpful in expressing the loneliness one feels. Later generations would listen to people like Nirvana and find in them an echo of their pain. I have always found it difficult finding words to communicate the experience of depression - they always fall short of the reality. In the reality of the experiences of others, I find their words resonate with my own life and experience.

JB Phillips, an Anglican priest and translator of the Bible, describes how when he was depressed he was asked to write down as best he could the intolerable pain he was suffering. He wrote the following:

'When this utterly overwhelming pain occurs it seems to me to be due to the simultaneous occurrence of the following four trains of thought. (Each by itself is nearly intolerable, but when all four attack together the unhappy self feels utterly overwhelmed.)

(a) Diminution of the personality. This is a slow but inevitable diminution of the self and it is apparently leading to its final extinction. All sorts of images of erosion may occur but they all point to one end: the final destruction of the personality. This is not a fear of death but a fear of being diminished to vanishing point so that one ceases to be anything at all.

(b) Alienation. This feeling can occur in a number of ways. Familiar things become somehow touched with horror, beauty in a work of music is discordant, even though some small part of oneself tries to reassure one that there is really beauty there. The sense of alienation means that one is not in one's own country, or has strayed into a strange country by mistake. Thus words have no meaning (as if a different language were spoken here): money has no value (as if an entirely different currency were in force). Everything is out of joint as though some sort of cosmic joke had altered the very nature of things.

(c) Self-condemnation. This is no rational weighing up of one's personal value. It is a roaring, galloping torrent of condemnation directed against the self's achievements. With remorseless energy this particular 'demon' rushes to and fro and up and down in one's mind, and with savage cruelty exposes everything that the self has done as being useless and worthless.

(d) Agony by comparison. The effect of this 'demon' is clearly an ally of the preceding one. But instead of reducing achievements to nothing it compares the prisoner's present miserable state with joyful states he has known before but which are utterly beyond his reach. If the memory is full (and it often is in this abnormal state), this is quite a long business. And since the most miserable of men usually has some streak of hope left in him he lets the process go on, hoping for some encouragement. But he is given instead an agony of comparison - the excruciating difference between his present condition and that which he enjoyed for many years. He may not, at any rate at first, be able to stop this fury of self-denigration but in time he may be able to see that it is irrational and learn firmly to switch it off.[2]

The sense of loneliness and isolation can be overwhelming and it is difficult to relate to others when in such a state. This leads to frustration in relationships and the sense of loneliness is further enforced. One feels useless and worthless. Everybody else, one imagines, is in a better state than s/he who is depressed and this leads to more bitter feelings. There is also associated with depression a harrowing anxiety. The smallest thing can cause an anxiety state and one is left overwhelmed by nervousness.

HA Williams, another Anglican vicar who shared his experience of depression [3] relates how even a little thing like taking a walk absolutely terrified him and how he had to take time before his confidence to do even this could return. I found

4

his experience resonated with my own. I often felt terror just going out for a walk or at having to preach, or meet someone. Another demon of depression is a sense of guilt, a feeling that one is completely unworthy of love. I have felt this too. Sometimes the whole state of depression can be so overwhelming that one only finds release in tears.

My own journey from depression and illness towards healing took place in a number of ways over a long period of time. One of the ways was the love of compassionate friends. These people managed to get through the wall of depression and helped restore in me some semblance of faith in humankind. Another way I was helped was by allowing myself to go into therapy. Therapists such as Robina and John helped me by their compassionate listening. One of the insights I got was in a form of therapy called psycho-drama. In the psycho-drama I relived an experience I had when I was young. This incident had poisoned my life and whenever I felt better it would cast its shadow over me and my world was once again dark. In the psycho-drama, the therapist, Suzy, said these simple words: 'You don't have to remain there.' It was as if I had been given permission to leave this particular event behind and rediscover the joy of ordinary things. Therapy and medical treatment were steps in my journey out of illness.

A second stage was the rediscovery of spirituality. Over all the years, even in the midst of the most profound darkness, I prayed even though God appeared to be distant. For me spirituality is concerned with prayer and contemplation. As Simon Tugwell points out, spirituality also involves a way of viewing things.[4] Spirituality is concerned with the way I see people and events and helps me cope with the confusions that are part of my life. My spirituality involves finding who I am before God, discovering his love for me and for all, and how to relate to my brothers and sisters.

My rediscovery of spirituality began with the experience of Jesus in Gethsemane as Mark relates it. This account goes as follows:

Gethsemane

'They came to a plot of land called Gethsemane, and he said to his disciples, "Stay here while I pray". Then he took Peter and James and John with him. And he began to feel terror and anguish. And he said to them, "My soul is sorrowful to the point of death. Wait here, and stay awake." And going on a little further he threw himself on the ground and prayed that, if it were possible, this hour might pass him by. "*Abba*, Father!" he said, "for you everything is possible. Take this cup away from me. But let it be as you, not I, would have."

'He came back and found them sleeping, and he said to Peter, "Simon are you asleep? Had you not the strength to stay awake one hour? Stay awake and pray not to be put to the test. The spirit is willing enough, but human nature is weak." Again he went away and prayed, saying the same words. And once more he came back and found them sleeping, their eyes were so heavy; and they could find no answer for him. He came back a third time and said to them, "You can sleep on now and have your rest. It is all over. The hour has come. Now the Son of man is to be betrayed into the hands of sinners. Get up! Let us go! My betrayer is not far away." ' (Mk:14:32-42)

Meditating on this passage led me to a rediscovery of such themes as loneliness, compassion and prayer, plus failed disciples. Later on in this work I share some meditations on these themes in relation especially to the Gospel of Mark. Often insights from other New Testament authors are included. From Mark I began to rediscover the other authors of the New-Testament, but before this I took an overall look at the Gospel of Mark to help me see these meditations in context.

An Overview of Mark

Mark's gospel may be taken as a literary whole. We are led to ask the questions: who is Jesus? Who do we say he is? Gethsemane is part of this literary whole. So in order to appreciate the Gethsemane scene in Mark, it is necessary to have some overall idea of Mark's gospel and what he is all about. It may well have been Paul who influenced Mark in giving the gospel its focus on the death of Jesus. Martin Kahler said the gospel was a passion narrative with an extended introduction. [5] JDG Dunn says it was Paul who first shaped and determined Christianity's distinctive category of 'gospel'. [6] The good news is Jesus, who acts in the love of God and invites others to join his company.

In the mid second century Justin (Trypho, 106.3) refers to 'Peter's Memoirs' being found in the gospel of Mark. Eusebius (EH 3.39.15-16) records an early 2nd century tradition about Mark that Papias received:

'Mark, having become the interpreter/translator of Peter, wrote down accurately, however, not in order, all that he recalled of what was either said or done by the Lord. For he had neither heard nor followed the Lord; but later (as I said) he followed Peter, who used to adapt his instruction to the needs of the moment or of the audience, but not with a view of making an orderly account of the Lord's sayings (logia). Accordingly Mark did no wrong in thus writing down some things as he recalled them, for he made it his aim to omit nothing he had heard and to state nothing therein falsely.

Such things did Papias recount of Mark.'

This Mark could well be the John Mark who is referred to as the cousin of Barnabas, (Acts 12:12) [7] and who quarrelled with Paul (Acts 15:36-40). In later years Mark was reconciled to Paul, later coming to Rome where he served Peter and Paul before their martyrdom.

Other authors (e.g. W Marxsen) argue for a different author and place of origin of Mark; [8] however nothing has been conclusively proven. For our purposes the tradition of Papias is sufficient. Mark, as one who served the Church in Rome, wrote for a community that suffered persecution and death - thus giving us another reason why Mark placed such emphasis on the cross in his gospel. Christ, too, suffered and those who followed him might face the same prospect. Through his gospel Mark helped to strengthen those who suffered.

The opening of Mark's gospel (Mk 1:1-15) presents the beginning of the gospel of Jesus as the fulfilment of Mal 3:1 and Isaiah 40:3. John the Baptist is the prophetic messenger crying in the wilderness to prepare the way of the Lord, the one who would baptise with the Holy Spirit. A voice from heaven, echoing Ps 2:7 and Is 42:1, speaks to Jesus as God's beloved Son and at his baptism the Spirit descends. Jesus goes into the desert where he is tempted. He then begins his ministry calling four men to be his followers and become fishers of people (1:16-20). In describing what appears to be the initial day of Jesus' ministry (1:21-38) Mark familiarizes the readers with the type of things done in proclaiming the kingdom: teaching in the Capernaum Synagogue with authority, exorcising an unclean spirit (the continued opposition of Satan), healing many people who were afflicted mentally or physically, and finally seeking a place to pray where he could be alone.

In 1:34 Jesus forbids the demons to speak 'because they know him'. This is the first instance of what scholars call Mark's 'Messianic Secret' whereby Jesus seems to hide his identity as the Son of God until this is made apparent after his death on the cross. Jesus' ministry then moves throughout Galilee (1:39-45). His ministry consists of preaching, driving out demons, and healings. 'Driving out demons' is the way a first century author would write; a modern author would emphasise the element of mental affliction and illness. Yet it is interesting that modern people still speak of 'confronting their demons', or 'exorcising their demons' as they seek mental health. Perhaps the first century language of Mark still speaks to us.

Then Mark narrates a set of controversies at Capernaum (2:1-3:6). Objections are raised by Scribes and Pharisees to Jesus' forgiving of sins, to his association with sinners, to the failure of the disciples to fast, and to their and his doing what was unlawful on the Sabbath. From a very early stage Jesus raises opposition which will eventually harden and lead to his violent death. John the Baptist, too, raises opposition because of his forthright speaking and is killed (6:14-29). In this way the reader is prepared for what will happen to Jesus.

Other accounts of Jesus' miracle workings are the curing of the daughter of Jairus and the woman with the flow of blood (5:21-43), the deaf mute (7:31-37), the blind man at Bethsaida (8.22-6), and the blind Bar-Timaeus (10:46-52). For Mark, these healings not only show that the time of salvation promised by the prophets have arrived (cf Is 35:4-6), but they also reveal the beginnings of a tendency which will become predominant in John: to see the mighty work as symbols of the post-resurrectional life offered to those who come to Jesus. Mark is eager to emphasise to the reader that Jesus is not just a charismatic wonder-worker. He is more than an Elijah or Elisha come back. He is Messiah and Son of God.

It is in 8:27-31 that we see Jesus take a different path from the charismatics of his own day. His disciples have been with Jesus from the start (see 3:13-39) and have seen his wonders. They probably shared the crowd's identification of Jesus as a prophet (8:28), but Peter goes on to identify Jesus as the Messiah (8:29). They are told to be silent about this, in the same way the demons were told to be quiet.

Then we come to the turning point in Mark's gospel where Jesus 'began to teach then that the Son of Man had to suffer much ...' (8:31). Peter had seen Jesus' healings and exorcisms and he had seen the so-called 'nature miracles' - the feeding of the multitudes (6:30-44, 8:1-10), the calming of the storm at sea (4:35-41) and the walking on water (6:45-52). Now he is not able to take on board that Jesus will suffer an ignominious fate. This failure to heed what Jesus says about suffering points to the fact that relations between Jesus and Peter and the other disciples were becoming increasingly strained. Jesus would repeat his warnings about his oncoming passion (9:30-32, 10:32-34), but the disciples misunderstood him. At Gethsemane (14:32-42) the disciples would sleep while Jesus was in agony, and at his arrest they would all desert him (14:50). Peter would deny he knew Jesus (14:66-72). The reader is prepared for this rupture in relationships by the misunderstanding of the disciples as Jesus foretold his passion.

* * * * *

The transfiguration (9:2-13) also produced a reaction that was another example of the inadequate faith of the disciples. Earlier in the gospel the identity of Jesus as God's Son was proclaimed during the baptism by a voice from heaven. The disciples were not present then and thus in the ministry of Jesus they had not heard the voice of God proclaim Jesus as His Son. Here Peter, James and John are with Jesus and they hear the voice proclaiming that Jesus is God's beloved Son. 'Listen to him,' (9:7) but they do not know what to do or say. In Gethsemane Peter, James and John will also be with Jesus - but now there is no heavenly voice and while Jesus is in deep distress they, unbelievably, sleep. They are totally insensitive to what is going on.

Jesus now sets his face towards Jerusalem [9] and on the way he heals Bar-Timaeus (10:46-52), who attempts to follow Jesus 'on the way'. 'The way' stands for the way to Jerusalem, but it can also be understood on a symbolic level. Following Jesus involved a conversion to him, often symbolized by leaving behind one's possessions (the rich young man, 10:17-22). It involved taking up one's cross and following Jesus (8:34). Following Jesus also implied sharing his ministry. Bar-Timaeus shared this willingness to follow Jesus 'on the way'. Underlying the children passage in 10:13-16, where Jesus welcomed the children while the disciples did not, this is the correction of a wrong attitude that demanded achievement, that sought status. Bar-Timaeus did not have an attitude that demanded achievement or sought status. He is in marked contrast to those closest to Jesus. For instance, the sons of Zebedee, James and John, ask Jesus for places of honour in his kingdom, one at his right hand and one at his left hand (10:35-

40). At the crucifixion the places at Jesus' right and left-hand would be taken by two thieves (15:27).

Jesus enters Jerusalem and is well received by the crowds (11:1-11). He is acclaimed by a hosanna cry of praise, by a line from Ps 118:26. A Markan intercalation ('sandwich') governs the next actions we see in Mark - the cursing of the fig tree, cleansing of the temple, and finding the fig tree withered (11:12-25). To curse the fig tree because it had no fruit seems to be an irrational act. Mark even reminds the reader that it was not the season for figs. However, the cursing of the fig tree is similar to the prophetic acts of the Old Testament whose very peculiarity attract attention to the message being presented (e.g. Jer 19:1-2, 10-11: Ez 12:1-7). The barren tree represents those authorities whose failures are evident in the action of the cleansing of the temple, which has been made a den of thieves instead of a house of prayer for all people (Jer 7:11; Is 56:7). This causes the Chief Priests and the Scribes to conspire and seek an opportunity to kill Jesus.

We then have the incident of the authorities questioning Jesus to catch him out. These incidents provide Jesus with an opportunity for teaching. In 12:1-12 he teaches the parable of wicked tenants who did not listen to the man who owned the vineyard and who eventually killed the son so that they might be in complete control. The authorities realized that it was they he was talking about and they sought even more to kill him.

In 13:1-13 Jesus delivers the last speech of his ministry that looks to the end-times, the final confrontation between good and evil. This is called the eschatological discourse, 'eschatological' referring to the end-times. This shows us that the oncoming events of the passion are to be understood in a deeper sense than just the death of one man. Jesus tells the disciples to stay awake (13:37). Yet when his agony began in Gethsemane, the disciples slept.

Jesus is now closer to his hour of pain and failure. His teaching had not been taken on board by those nearest him. The initial enthusiasm of the crowd for Jesus, after his miracles, had waned. Judas, one of the twelve disciples, would even go on to betray Jesus (14:10-11). Jesus' dark night was just beginning. In Gethsemane we see clearly his loneliness and depression.

In the little scene at Bethany, a nameless woman is more perceptive than anyone else and she seeks to console Jesus (14:3-9). She pours onto his head the contents of a jar of very precious ointment, thus silently stating her recognition of him as the 'anointed messiah'. The disciples, the twelve, are irritated by this act, even though some had been present at the transfiguration. This indicates once again the disharmony in the relationships between Jesus and those closest to him. Jesus silences them, saying: 'She has done what she could: she has anointed my body beforehand for its burial'. (14:8) These are some of the loneliest words of Jesus. The nameless woman was aware of the fate Jesus was facing and sought to console him. The apostles were in denial, locked in a world of incomprehension.

In the scene of the last supper we have the drama of the self-giving of Jesus. He took the bread and said, 'This is my body' (14:22). In the same way he took the cup of wine and he said to them: 'This is my blood.' (14:24) Jesus showed he was laying down his life for others. His sacrifice was total.

Things happen rapidly after this. Jesus returns to Gethsemane where he prays in agony (14:32-42). He asks the disciples to remain with him and he takes Peter, James and John aside, but they sleep. Jesus in his prayer does not hear the voice of God, who is silent. Yet Jesus ultimately receives strength and is prepared for the oncoming trial. The disciples do not pray and when the arresting party come they scatter (14:50). Jesus is betrayed by Judas, who kisses him, and is seized by the mob. At this point Mark introduces a surreal effect. A young man appears wearing a linen cloth. The mob grab him and he runs away naked (14:51-52). He epitomizes the confusion and pain of the events taking place.

In rapid succession after this we have the trial before the Sanhedrin, (14:53-65), Peter's denial (14:66-72). Peter had promised that even if all fell away he would not deny Jesus (14:29) but when the hour came he was afraid and disowned Jesus. Jesus is crowned with thorns (15:16-20). He is mocked as king of the Jews. There is bitter irony here. The soldiers were nearer the truth than they realized. He was truly the king of the Jews.

Jesus is condemned to death and led to Golgotha where he is crucified between two thieves. On the cross he cries out in a loud voice '*Eloi, Eloi, lama Sabachthani?*' which means 'My God, why have you forsaken me?' (15:34) This is at once a cry of agony and, as we shall see later when we look at Jesus and lament, a cry of trust. Then with a loud cry Jesus dies (15:37). The centurion standing at the foot of the cross, observing all that has happened, says: 'In truth this man was Son of God.' (15:39) Jesus is now identified. The cross represents the most authentic moment in Jesus' life where he gives himself totally so that we might believe.

Standing by the cross are Mary of Magdala, Mary the mother of James the younger and Joset, and Salome (15:40-41). They will be important in the next scene. They take note of where Jesus is buried. They return to the tomb when the Sabbath is over (16:1-8). When they get to the tomb they find the stone rolled away and a young man clothed in a white robe sitting in the tomb. The calm demeanour of this young man contrasts with the scene of the young man who ran away naked (15:51f).

He tells the women that Jesus is risen and he is gone before them into Galilee. They are to tell the apostles, and especially Peter, this. The scene is calm and tranquil but it would not be in character for Mark to leave it like this. The endings of Mark's gospel (16:6-20) were added later. [10] This means that the gospel ended at 16:8: '... and they said nothing to anyone because they were afraid.' The women showed themselves also as fallible followers. I will discuss 16:8 later on in my work.

What we see in Mark's picture of Jesus is one who was the Son of God. He showed himself to be so in his healings of broken bodies and spirits. He offered defenceless and unconditional love which led to his rejection and death but he did not withdraw his love and he was vindicated by God the Father, who brought him to the resurrection. His offer of defenceless love is still there as is shown when the offer of reconciliation is proffered to Peter and the others. We are offered the same love when we come to meet Jesus.

Where is the Joy?

I remember once hearing an interview with the playwright Tennessee Williams. I had always admired him, but at the same time I always found his characters to be terribly sad. I was always left with an incredible sense of sorrow after watching one of his plays. In the interview he was asked why did he not write plays about happy people. He remarked that if he ever met a happy person then he would write about a happy person. For many years I felt much the same way. I found consolation in returning to Mark's Gethsemane scene with all its rawness. There I found that I was not alone and found strength to carry on. One question many people asked me, however, was: where is the joy? As I showed earlier, the words 'You don't have to stay there' were a revelation to me as I was beginning to come to terms with traumas of the past. Through a combination of events I began to see that my spiritual journey to healing required me to look again at the idea of joy.

Mark's gospel is sombre in tone. The shadow of the cross is found right throughout his gospel. Other New Testament writers, such as Paul, bring out the importance of the resurrection. Mark, on the other hand, doesn't have any resurrection appearance, the emphasis definitely being on the death of Jesus as the most authentic moment of his life. Yet Mark begins his gospel with the words: 'The beginning of the good news about Jesus Christ, the Son of God' (1:1). The good news is revealed in Jesus himself because he reveals the healing power of God for those afflicted in mind and body.

He brings hope to those on the margins of society and he calls the disciples to share in his ministry. He is an example of defenceless, generous love, yet he is rejected and subjected to a violent, shameful death.

Yet the story does not end there: he is raised from the dead and offers reconciliation to those who had denied him. He had moved from the pain of Gethsemane and Golgotha to transformed life. It is in following this path of Jesus that I came to the light of a new day. It is to St Francis that I look to find an understanding of joy.

The story of St Francis and 'perfect joy' is one with which I have wrestled for a long time. In the story of 'Perfect Joy,' St Francis finds himself on the road with Brother Leo and is to be found in the 'Little Flowers of St Francis'. The conversation between the two begins as follows:

'One winter day St Francis was coming to St Mary of the Angels from Perugia with Brother Leo, and the bitter cold made them suffer keenly. St Francis called to Brother Leo, who was walking a bit ahead of him, and he said: 'Brother Leo, even if the Friars Minor in every country give a great example of holiness and integrity and good edification, nevertheless write down and note carefully that perfect joy is not in that.'

And when he had walked on a bit, St Francis called him again, saying: 'Brother Leo, even if a Friar Minor gives sight to the blind, heals the paralysed, drives out devils, gives hearing back to the deaf, makes the lame walk, and restores speech to the dumb, and what is still more, brings back to life a man who has been dead four days, write that perfect joy is not in that.'

Their conversation continues along the same lines. Saint Francis tells Leo that if the Friars Minor, that is, St Francis' brothers, were versed in all knowledge, including the Christian Scriptures, then perfect joy would not be found there. If a brother of Saint Francis could speak with the voice of angels and knew about the course of the stars and the healing powers of herbs, if he understood the things of nature, he retorts that perfect joy would not be found there. If the Friars Minor should perform great works of conversion, that perfect joy would not be there. The bemused Leo asks: 'Where then can perfect joy be found?'

And St Francis replied: 'When we come to St Mary of the Angels, soaked by the rain and frozen by the cold, all soiled with mud and suffering from hunger, and we ring at the gate of the place and the brother porter comes and says angrily, "Who are you?" and we say, "We are two of your brothers"; and he contradicts us, saying, "You are not telling the truth. Rather, you are two rascals who go around deceiving people and stealing what they give to the poor. Go away!" And he does not open for us, but makes us stand outside in the snow and rain, cold and hungry, until night falls - then if we endure all those insults and cruel rebuffs patiently, without being troubled and without complaining, and if we reflect humbly and charitably that the porter really knows us and that God makes him speak against us, oh, Brother Leo, write that perfect joy is there!

'And if we continue to knock, and the porter comes out in anger, and drives us away with curses and hard blows like bothersome scoundrels, saying, "Get away from here, you dirty thieves - go to the hospital! Who do you think you are? You certainly won't eat or sleep here!" - and if we bear it patiently and take the insults with joy and love in our hearts, oh, Brother Leo, write that that is perfect joy!

'And if later, suffering intensely from hunger and the painful cold, with night falling, we still knock and call, and crying loudly beg them to open for us and let us come in for the love of God, and he grows still more angry and says, "Those fellows are bold and shameless ruffians. I'll give them what they deserve!" and he comes out with a knotty club, and grasping us by the cowl throws us onto the ground, rolling us in the mud and snow, and beats us with that club so much that he covers our bodies with wounds - if we endure all those evils and insults and blows with joy and patience, reflecting that we must accept and bear the sufferings of the Blessed Christ patiently for love of Him, oh, Brother Leo, write: that is perfect joy!' (Little Flowers of Saint Francis, Ch 8).

16

I remember once finding myself lost in a little Italian town. I came upon a church and said to myself that I would be able to get directions there. I saw a brother sweeping in the church and I approached him. He grunted at me and then ignored me. The sentiment that came to mind was not 'perfect joy'.

Indeed there are many more important situations in life where I do not think that the term 'perfect joy' belongs, not just my little incident of being lost. Horrific events like Auschwitz, Rwanda and Bosnia cast a long shadow over the 20th century. In ordinary life the way people abuse each other is becoming more highlighted today. Abuse can be verbal, emotional and/or psychological, physical and sexual. There are many ways we hurt each other. Indeed not a few people have found themselves so diminished that they took their own lives. In the face of this immense sea of hurt, sayings like 'perfect joy', 'it's the will of God' or 'these things were sent to try us' sound cynical and hollow. Yet it is worth staying with St Francis to glean what we can about our attitude to suffering.

The first example, I consider, is the stigmata of Saint Francis. This refers to the wounds of Christ that appear on Saint Francis. The stigmata are not necessarily a sign of sanctity. It was over the whole span of his life that this epithet was applied to Francis. Saint Bonaventure wrote a biography of St Francis in which he spoke of how the saint received the stigmata. He tells how Francis meditated on the passion of Jesus. Jesus was for Saint Francis the revelation of God himself. He showed in his life the love, compassion and vulnerability of God. This love led to Jesus' rejection and violent death, yet he continued to love and was vindicated in His resurrection. On Mount La Verna, when Francis was praying, he received the marks of Christ on his body. Dante, in his 'Paradiso', says that this sign was 'the final seal received from Christ and borne by his limbs for two years when it pleased God, who had given him such good, to draw him up to the reward he deserved by making him humble' (Dante, *Divina Commedia*, Paradiso, XI. 106-11).

John of the Cross meditated on the stigmata in his work *Living Flame of Love* and his insight is penetrating. John distinguishes between a purely internal cauterization of the soul affected solely by the Holy Spirit and 'another and most sublime way' of burning in which the soul is wounded internally in such a way that the flame of divine love fills it so entirely so that 'it seems to the soul that the whole universe is a sea of love in which it is swallowed'. In this latter case God may allow the effect of this interior love to pass outward into the senses, 'as was the case when the seraph wounded St Francis: when the soul is wounded by love with five wounds, the effects extend to the body and the wounds are marked on the body, and it is wounded just as the soul is'. (*Living Flame of Love*, 2:10). For John priority is always given to the invisible interior wound.

It was in a spirit of love that Francis bore the stigmata. He saw in Jesus' journey from Gethsemane to Calvary, leading to Easter day, a sign of the love God has for us. He accompanied Jesus in spirit on that journey, suffering with Him but coming to a newer and deeper love and compassion for all. It was in this spirit of love that Francis could speak of 'perfect joy'. Every event was an opportunity for him to be with Christ on his journey from Gethsemane to Easter day. He came through the events of his life to a deeper more compassionate love for God and all creation. Through his wounds he became a wounded healer for his brothers and sisters. He embraced all people in his love, which reflected the love of Christ. He tells us in his Testament that at one time the sight of lepers nauseated him but God led him into their presence where he welcomed them as brothers and sisters. He saw the person of Christ in those who suffered from leprosy and all those who are outsiders, for whatever reason. He had compassion for all people and all creation.

His vision of Christ, as revealing the love of the Father, shows us that the God of Francis was a vulnerable God who cared for his sons and daughters. Thomas of Celano, Francis' first biographer, quotes Francis as saying: 'The love of him who loved us much is such to be loved.' (2 Cel 196) The Love which we receive draws a response of love from our hearts. We return love in return for love. This is put even more forcefully in a prayer attributed to Saint Francis called 'The Absorbeat'. It reads:

'May the power of your love, O Lord, fiery and sweet as honey, wean my heart from all that is under heaven, so that I may die for love of your love, you who were so good as to die for love of my love'.

Thomas Aquinas would later speak of God as being thirsty for our love. God comes across in all this as one who loves his children and is vulnerable. He hopes to receive our love freely given. As Francis put it: Jesus died for love of our love.

Thus it was love that touched the heart of Francis and he worked through his painful experiences in a spirit of love. Every event was an opportunity for him to enter into a more loving relationship with God. This showed itself in the love and compassion he had in his life. There is still one more instance that brings this point out even more clearly.

The 'Mirror of Perfection' (par:100), tells the story of how Francis at one time was very ill and suffered gravely with his eyes. He was also afflicted by a plague of mice in his cell. The picture one gets here is one of inhuman suffering. Francis was depressed and began to feel sorry for himself, but he rediscovered his love for God and allowed that to permeate his life. In this state he sang of the beauty of God and prayed for all his creation. One must remember that in all this Francis was practically blind and his illness caused him to be confined. The 'Canticle of Brother Sun' is the name given to the canticle Francis composed. It begins as follows:

'Praised be you, My Lord, with all your creatures,
especially Sir Brother Sun,
who is the day and through whom you enlighten us.
And he is beautiful and shining with great splendour,
Of you, Most High, he bears the likeness.
Praised be you, My Lord, through Sister Moon and the stars,
In heaven you formed them shining and precious and beautiful.'

Francis' blindness and illness were permeated with love and became the opportunity for him to praise and love even more.

The picture of Saint Francis that emerges here is that of a very strong character totally wrapped in love. There is still another story of Saint Francis which showed he had to struggle before he could realize his vision. Thomas of Celano in his biography, and the 'Mirror of Perfection' tell us of a time when Saint Francis was mentally afflicted. Those who suffer their own Gethsemane experiences can relate here to what Francis went through. 'The Mirror of Perfection' (par:99) tells us of a time when Francis was sorely tempted. He began to withdraw from his brothers because he was so sad. Thomas of Celano tells us that Francis was filled with sorrow and would weep bitterly. Those who have undergone illness or depression can relate to this. The love of God which Francis celebrated in his life seemed to be removed from him and he was in darkness. His was truly a Gethsemane experience, but he was to be led through this to a deeper love. Celano tells us:

'After being thus assailed for several years, he was praying one day at St Mary of the Portiuncula when he heard a voice within his spirit saying: "Francis, if you have faith like a mustard seed, you will say to this mountain: 'Remove from here', and it will remove." The saint replied: "Lord, what mountain do you want me to remove?" And again he heard: "The mountain is your temptation." And weeping, Francis said, "Let it be unto me, Lord, as you have said." Immediately all the temptation was driven out, and he was made free and put completely at peace within himself.' (2 Cel 115)

His depression was where he met God. He was led through this experience to peace.

Francis' spirit of joy has biblical roots. In the letter to the Philippians Paul uses the words *chara* (joy) and *chairein* (rejoice) fourteen times and it is an important theme in this letter. In the letter when Paul spoke of joy he was describing a settled state of mind characterized by peace (*eirene*). [11] This peace came from their experience of God. They trusted themselves to this love, hoping it would lead them through their trials to a deeper relationship with him.

Francis' spirit of joy helps me put my Gethsemane experience into perspective. In reading and contemplating Mark's account the readers come to realize that they are the ones who keep vigil with Christ. The disciples slept. Jesus' undergoing of mental pain teaches us we are not alone. He was in that place before us and he shares our pain. We also learn that he empowers us with his love and compassion to work through our experience to come to a new day. I am not writing as one who is totally healed, but as who is on the way.

I still get times of darkness and confusion but once again I return to Gethsemane to keep vigil with Christ. As TS Eliot said:

'We shall not cease from exploration
And the end of all our exploring
Will be to arrive where we started
And know the place for the first time.'
(Little Gidding)

NOTES ON CHAPTER 1

1. K Seybold and U Mueller, *Sickness and Healing* (USA Abingdon Press, 1978-81), p44-46
2. JB Phillips, *The Price of Success* (London: Hodder and Stoughton. 1984), ch14
3. HA Williams, *Some Day I'll Find You* (London: Fount Paperbacks, 1982) p166-173
4. S Tugwell, *Ways of Imperfection*, (London: Darton, Longman and Todd, 1984), pVII f.
5. M Kahler, *The So-Called Historic Jesus and the Historic Biblical Christ* (Philadephia: Fortress Press: 1956 edtion, originally published 1896) p80 n11.
6. JDG Dunn, *The Theology of Paul the Apostle* (Edinburgh: T&T, Clark 1998) p232f
7. See my *Catch the Wind* (London: Pen Press, 1996), p63-73.

8. For a review of the problem of the authorship of Mark see PJ Achtemeir, *Gospel of Mark*, ABD, IV, 542-544. RE Brown sees value in the Papias tradition and I follow him; see R.E. Brown, *Introduction to the New Testament* (London: Doubleday, 1996), p158-161

9. For a discussion of the journey motif in Mark cf. W Kelber, *The Kingdom in Mark: A New Place and a New Time* (Philadelphia: Fortress Press, 1976) p67-85. E Manicardi, *Il Cammino di Gesu nel Vangelo di Marco* (Rome: Biblical Institute Press, 1981)

10. See V Taylor, *The Gospel According to St Mark* (London: Macmillan, 1996 edition), p610-615: B Metzger, *A Textual Commentary on the Greek New Testament* (United Bible Societies, 1975) p126-128

11. GF Hawthorn, *Philippians: Word Biblical Commentary 43* (USA Word, in., 1983) p18

Quotations about St. Francis can be found in *St. Francis of Assisi, Omnibus of Sources,* Marion A. Halig (ed.), (Chicago: Franciscan Herald Press, 1983)

CHAPTER 2
THE WOUNDED HEALER: COMPASSION

'And we are put on earth a little space,
that we may learn to bear the beams of love.'
(William Blake)

Jesus, the compassion of God

In the Old Testament God is portrayed as the faithful lover of Israel and the relationship between God and the human person is expressed in terms of love. In the Song of Songs there is no separation between human and divine love. Here lovemaking conjures up sensual images of perfume, wine, spices, gazelles, honeycomb, pomegranate, candlelight, dancing and glad songs.

Love imagery is an important motif in the prophets as well. Using the imagery of husband and wife, parent and child, Yahweh is seen as a zealous, unfailing and compassionate lover, one who will not withdraw his love because of infidelity and rejection. The prophets characterise the divine-human relationship as a love affair or marriage. Israel is often portrayed as a faithless bride to whom Yahweh remains loving and faithful (Hos, 1-3; 4:18; 11:1; Jer 2:2-25; 3:1-13; Ez 16; 23:1-49; Isa 54:4-10; 62:4-5).

God's love in the Old Testament is made visible in His unfailing and loving activity in Israel's life - the Exodus, the gifts of the land and the Torah. In Deuteronomy God's love provides the motive for Israel to love God (7:6-11) 'You shall love the Lord, your God, with all your heart and with all your soul and all your might' (Deut 6:5). For Israel, love involved not only sensuality and affection, but also ethical love of neighbour and fidelity to the covenant and love.

The psalmist describes God's love is this way:

'The Lord is gracious and merciful, slow to anger and abounding in steadfast love. The Lord is good to all, and his compassion is over all that he has made' (Ps1 45:8-9).

The Hebrew word for compassion (*Rahamin*) expresses the empathetic attachment of one being to another. This feeling of attachment, in Semitic thought, has its origins in the experience of maternity, or also the entrails (or gut). Etymologically the Hebrew word for compassion means 'trembling womb' [1.] Thus the mother's intimate relationship with her child is the prime image for understanding the nature of compassion. Isaiah uses this image when he says:

'Zion was saying, Yahweh has abandoned me, the Lord has forgotten me. Can a woman forget her baby at the breast, feel no pity for the child she has borne? Even if these were to forget, I shall not forget you. Look, I have engraved you on the palms of my hands, your ramparts are ever before me' (Is 49:14-16).

The implication of all this is that the mother's physical and pathological bond with her child provides the basis for the development for the more abstract notions of compassion, pity, mercy and tenderness.

In this way, compassion may be understood as the capacity to be attracted and moved by the fragility, weakness and suffering of another. It is the ability to be vulnerable enough to undergo risk and loss for the good of another. Compassion involves a movement to help the other; it also involves a movement of participation in the experience of the other in order to be present and available in solidarity and communion. Compassion involves sensitivity to the one who is weak and vulnerable, wounded. It also involves the vulnerability to be affected by the other. One's deepest inner feelings lead one to compassionate acts of mercy and kindness.

In the New Testament the author of the letter to the Hebrews introduces Jesus as follows:

24

'At various times in the past and in various different ways, God spoke to our ancestors through the prophets; but in our own time, the last days, he has spoken to us through his Son, the Son that he has appointed to inherit everything and through whom he made everything there is. He is the radiant light of God's glory and the perfect copy of his nature, sustaining the universe by his powerful command, and now that he has destroyed the defilement of sin, he has gone to take his place in heaven at the right hand of divine Majesty. So he is now as far above the angels as the title which he has inherited is higher than their own name.' (Heb 1:1-4)

The author draws on wisdom - motifs of the Old Testament. Wisdom is presented as the existent heavenly figure present with God as his master - an artisan (Prov. 8:30), by whom God laid the foundations of the world (Prov. 3:19). Wisdom is the sustainer and governor of the universe (Wis 8:1) and she is described, in words similar to those used of the Son in Hebrews, as a reflection of eternal light and an unspoiled mirror of the working of God and an image of his goodness (Wis 7:26).

Paul too, writes of the Son as an agent in creation (Cor 8:6) and in the letter to the Colossians, the Son is spoken of as the image of God (Col 1:15). The fourth evangelist, writing later, uses ideas, all of which can be paralleled in the wisdom literature, to describe the Son under the form of the Word (Logos).

From this we gather a sense of Jesus as one who reveals God in a unique way. In Mark's gospel we hear God at Jesus' baptism at the hands of John the Baptist: 'You are my Son, the Beloved; my favour rests on you' (MK 1:11) and at the transfiguration the three, Peter, James and John hear the voice of God who tells them: 'This is my Son, the beloved. Listen to him' (9:7). The God revealed by Jesus is the God of the Old Testament who has compassion for all his creation (Ps 145:9). In Luke we hear Jesus say 'Be compassionate, just as your Father is compassionate' (Lk 6:36). In Jesus this compassion is seen and experienced.

In the gospels there is an expression which we come across twelve times and is used exclusively to describe Jesus or his Father. That expression is 'to be moved with compassion'. The Greek verb *splangchmizomai* reveals to us the deep and powerful meaning of the expression. The *spangchna* are the entrails of the body, or as we might say today the gut or guts. This translates the Hebrew word for compassion (*Rahamin*). For the authors of the New Testament the gut signifies the place where our most intimate and intense emotions are located. They are the centre from which passionate love or passionate hate grow. When the Gospels speak of Jesus as being moved in the entrails or guts, they are speaking of something deep, passionate and mysterious. All their feelings, emotions and passions are one in divine love. When Jesus was moved to compassion, the source of all life trembled, the ground of all love burst open and the abyss of God's immense, inexhaustible and unfathomable tenderness revealed itself in him.

Jesus' compassion is made visible in the healing stories of the New Testament. When Jesus saw the blind, the paralysed and the sick being brought to him he felt compassion for them, he was moved within and experienced the pain of others in his own heart. When he noticed the thousands who had followed him for days and were tired and hungry he was moved with compassion (Mk 8:2). So it was with the blind Bar-Timaeus (Mk 10:46-52). All these people moved him. He felt their pain in the depth of his being. He could be compassionate with the lost, the hungry and the sick. He sensed the pain of these people with a perfect sensitivity. The great mystery revealed to us is that Jesus chose in freedom to suffer our pains. In him we grow to accept ourselves as the persons we truly are. Jesus' compassion for us who are the sick and the lonely ones makes it possible for us to face our broken selves and in our time of brokenness find a cause of hope not despair.

In the Gospel of Mark, which I mainly use as the basis for my meditations, we find an instructive little story of Jesus' compassion.

26

'A man suffering from a virulent skin disease came to him and pleaded on his knees saying, "If you are willing, you can cleanse me." Feeling sorry for him, Jesus stretched out his hand, touched him and said to him, "I am willing. Be cleansed." At once the skin disease left him and he was cleansed. And at once Jesus sternly charged him, and sent him away at once and said to him, "Mind you tell no one anything, but go and show yourself to the priests, and make the offering for your cleansing prescribed by Moses as evidence to them." The man went away, but then started freely proclaiming and divulging the story everywhere, so that Jesus could no longer go openly into any town, but had to stay outside in deserted places. Even so, people from all around kept coming to him.' (1:40-45)

We are told Jesus 'feeling sorry for him' healed the leper. 'Feeling sorry for him' can also be translated as 'moved with compassion', as we saw above. However in some manuscripts we are told that Jesus was angry, not that he felt sorry for the leper. What would have caused such a reaction in Jesus? Surely not the approach of the leper whom he healed. CE Cranfield [2] suggests as a possibility that this anger was anger in a general way, his reaction to the foul disease which caused so much suffering. It could also be anger with Satan at his disfiguring of God's creatures. Both ideas of being moved by compassion or being angry at the sad state of the leper evoke the idea of Jesus being moved in the depths of his being by the pain and isolation of the leper.

In Chapter 10 of Mark we see Jesus express more tender feelings. This comes from discussion with the young rich man. We are told that Jesus looked steadily at him and loved him (10:21). However, the rich man cannot find it in himself to respond and leave his wealth behind. He goes away sad.

In the Gethsemane scene Mark uses an economy of words to express Jesus' state of mind in the garden. The words come as a sharp shock. We are told that Jesus began 'to be greatly distraught and troubled'. (14:33b). This graphically describes the change in Jesus' state as he approached his final hours. The Greek word for 'greatly distraught' is *ekthambeisthai* and the word for 'troubled' is *ademonein*.

The state of Jesus recalls the suffering servant of Deutero-Isaiah. In fact the theme of the one who 'was despised, the lowest of man, a man of sorrows, acquainted with grief', which is found in Deutero-Isaiah (Is 53:3), is present in the whole Passion-narrative. Isaiah goes on to describe the suffering servant as the one who bears our sufferings:

'Yet ours were the sufferings he was bearing, ours the sorrows he was carrying; we thought of him as someone being punished and struck with affliction by God whereas he was being wounded for our rebellions, crushed because of our guilt; the punishment reconciling us fell on him, and we have been healed by his bruises. We had all gone astray like sheep, each taking his own way, and Yahweh brought the acts of rebellion of all of us to bear on him. Ill-treated and afflicted, he never opened his mouth, like a lamb led to the slaughterhouse, like a sheep dumb before its shearers he never opened his mouth.' (Is: 53:4-7)

In Mark's description of Jesus in Gethsemane the image of the suffering servant is evoked. Joel Marcus shows that the test of Isaiah finds expression in Jesus' passion:[3]

Mark		Isaiah
14:10-11, 18,21	handing over	53:6 12
41-42, 44; 15:1, 10, 15		
14:24	blood poured out for many	53:12
14:61; 15:5	silence before accusers	53:7
14:65	spitting, slapping	50:6
15:5; 39	amazement of nations and kings	52:15
15:6-15	criminal saved, innocent man delivered to murder	53:6,12

Vincent Taylor says that both words *ekthambeisthai* and *ademonein* emphasise the strongest and deepest of feelings.[4] They depict the utmost degree of horror and suffering. *Thambeisthai* occurs in 1:27 where it means 'to be amazed'.

Ekthambeisthai came from this word and it has the sense of 'shuddering awe'. Swete [5] says that the word means 'terrified surprise'. Taylor enumerates different translations for *ekthambeisthai* which, taken together, help convey the sense of what is going on for Jesus. The revised version translates it as 'greatly amazed', RSV as 'greatly distressed', Moffat as 'appalled' and Torrey as 'deeply agitated'. To this list can be added the Jerusalem Bible translation, which reads 'terror'.

Ademonein is also used in Phil 2:6 where it means to be 'sorely troubled', Swete [6] says that the verb expresses the distress that follows a great shock. JB Lightfoot [7] says that *ademonein* describes the confused, half-disorientated state which is produced by physical derangement, or by a mental state such as grief, shame or disappointment. Taylor also provides a list of possible translations.

The revised version translates it as 'sore-troubled, RSV as 'troubled', Moffat as 'agitated' and Weymouth as 'to be full of distress'. The Jerusalem Bible translates it as 'anguish'. Taylor goes on to say: 'With every desire to avoid unwarranted psychological interpretations, it is impossible to do any kind of justice to Mark's words without seeing in them something of the astonishment of the Son of Man who knows that He is also the suffering Servant of Isa. 1iii. It is too little observed that the description and the saying which follows belong to the brief interval before Jesus leaves His three disciples. The intensity of the anguish drives him from them to seek peace before the face of His Father.' [8]

In being compassionate and loving Jesus had left himself totally vulnerable. Now the full weight of rejection and open hatred was upon him. This left him in deep distress as he faced the oncoming passion. Failure was very real for him.

One of the most powerful experiences in a life of compassion is the expansion of the heart into a world-embracing space of healing from which no-one is excluded. Jesus embraced this in his life. He saw his compassion rejected. All that was left was rejection, anguish and terror. I find a letter written by Vincent Van Gogh to his brother illuminating at this point. Van Gogh says:

'There may be a great fire in our soul, yet no one ever comes to warm himself at it, and the passers-by only see a wisp of smoke coming through the chimney, and go along their way. Look here, now, what must be done? Must one tend the inner fire, have salt in oneself, wait patiently yet with how much impatience for the hour when somebody will come and sit down near it - maybe to stay? Let him who believes in God wait for the hour that will come sooner or later.' [9]

Van Gogh was on fire with passion and love. This expressed itself in his art. Yet he was not appreciated and had to wait patiently until others shared his vision, which he did not see happen in his lifetime. Jesus too was alive with love and strong compassionate feelings. All he could do was pray that he would be heard. But now all was silent. The disciples slept. Jesus was faced with his own anguish and distress. It was in this state that he prayed.

The letter to the Hebrews provides interesting insights into Jesus and his compassion. The letter was written independently of Mark. We hear the author tell us:

'Therefore he had to become like his brothers and sisters in every respect, so that he might be a merciful and faithful high priest in the service of God, to make a sacrifice of atonement for the sins of the people. Because he himself was tested by what he suffered, he is able to help those who are being tested' (Heb 2:17-18).

In the thought of the author of the letter to the Hebrews Jesus is taken up into God's presence where he continues his ministry of prayer on behalf of his brothers and sisters. This leads the author to develop his theology of Jesus as the supreme high-priest. To be compassionate with his brothers and sisters he became like them in every respect. As Gregory of Nazianzus later remarked, 'what is not assumed is not healed'. This Jesus represents to his brothers and sisters in relation to God. He carries their pains, struggles and failures to the heart of God. He suffered and was tempted and therefore he is able to help those who are tempted. In Chapter 4 the author returns to the same themes. He says:

'Since, then, we have a great high-priest who has passed through the heavens, Jesus, the Son of God, let us hold fast to our confession. For we do not have a high priest who is unable to sympathize with our weaknesses, but we have one who in every respect has been tested as we are, yet without sin. Let us therefore approach the throne of grace with boldness, so that we may receive mercy and find grace to help in time of need.' (Hebrews 4:14-16)

Jesus is here described as 'Son of God', the one who suffers because he has, through common experience, a real kinship with those who suffer. His temptations had not been confined to certain compartments of his life (eg to those temptations which are specially mentioned in the gospels), but they covered the entire range of human experience. The author can truthfully say that Jesus was tempted yet did not sin. Precisely because Christians have a compassionate high-priest they have grounds for confident assurance that the barriers between God and men and women have been broken down and we are accepted by God. God sees and loves in us what he sees and loves in Jesus, our compassionate high-priest.

Hebrews 5:7-10 is interesting for a discussion of Jesus. Raymond Brown [10] argues that Hebrews 5:7-10 forms another witness from another tradition to the events of Gethsemane. It is independent of Mark, thus enabling us to argue that the events of Gethsemane were historical, and treasured in the different traditions of the early communities. The pericope tells us:

'In the days of his flesh, Jesus offered up prayers and supplications, with loud cries and tears, to the one who was able to save him from death, and he was heard because of his reverent submission. Although he was a Son, he learned obedience through what he suffered; and having been made perfect, he became the source of eternal salvation for all who obey him, having been designated by God a high priest according to the order of Melchizedek'. (Hebrews 5:7-10)

The author proves the human suffering by reference to an incident in the days of the earthly life of Jesus, the incident in the Garden of Gethsemane. We are told Jesus offered up prayers and supplications. The word *prosenegkos,* translated as 'offered', implies that Christ's agony in Gethsemane was representative, bringing before God the pleadings of men and women in their hour of desperate need. Prayers and supplications stress Jesus' reaction to his situation. Jesus prayed for himself to be saved from death. Mark 14:36 tells us that Jesus said, 'Take this cup from me'. The petition was not granted but he was heard and he was set free from fear. At the end of the scene in Gethsemane we see Jesus once more in control of himself as he tells the disciples to get up, his enemy is at hand (Mk 14:42).

It was precisely because his prayer was not granted that although he was Son, he learned obedience from what he suffered. He learnt to submit himself to the events from which he wanted to be freed. The word 'obedience' may often evoke negative feelings and ideas. We think of orders we follow because we cannot refuse. We think of doing things others say are good for us but whose value we do not see. None of these negative associations apply to the obedience of Jesus. His obedience is listening to God's loving word and responding to it, knowing that in the end he will be vindicated by this same God in spite of the prospect of imminent failure and catastrophe.

Jesus took his obedience up to death (Phil 2:8), to the point beyond which it could be taken no further. The idea of Christ being made perfect, in the thought of the author of the letter to the Hebrews, involved Christ, through his sufferings, achieving his end or goal, fulfilling his mission on earth. [11] He has been raised by God and is now alive in his presence where he is a high priest of the order of Melchizedeck. The agony of Gethsemane and Calvary gives rise to Easter Day.

The Wounded Healer

When I think of suffering I think of the fury of Ivan Karamazov in Dostoyevsky's *The Brothers Karamazov.*

He rebels against the idea that our sufferings are to be endured for the sake of the perfect harmony and bliss which will be ours hereafter:

'But, objects Ivan, if all must suffer to pay for the eternal harmony, why is it necessary to force innocent children into the scheme? A poor child of five was subjected to every possible torture by her cultivated parents. They beat her, thrashed her, kicked her for no reason till her body was one bruise. Then they went to greater refinements of cruelty - shut her up all night in the cold and frost in a privy. The final harmony is not worth the tears of one tortured child who beats itself on the breast with its little fist and prays in its stinking outhouse, with its unexpiated tears, to 'dear kind God'! It's not worth it ... If the sufferings of children go to swell the sum of sufferings which is necessary to pay for the truth, then I protest that the truth is not worth such a price ... I don't want harmony. For love for humanity I don't want it ... And so I hasten to give back my entrance ticket, and if I am an honest man I am bound to give it back as soon as possible. And that I am doing. It's not God I don't accept, only I most respectfully return him the ticket.' [12]

So much suffering in our world dehumanises and destroys. It is against this that Ivan is rebelling. Ivan's speech was so strong that Dostoyevsky himself was frightened and had to ask himself whether he would be able to come up with an answer. 'Nowhere in Europe,' he said, 'is so powerful a defence of atheism to be found. My own belief in Christ and confession of him are thus not those of a simple child. My hosanna has emerged from a crucible of doubt.' [13]

Dostoyevsky's answer does not take the form of a point by point refutation of Christian arguments. He presents the readers not with a reasoning process but with a human being. This is the monk Zossima - his life, his practice, his love. Zossima had arrived at this compassionate self by working through the mistakes and pain of his own life. Those who come to him experience the healing power of his love and understanding. He is the Christ figure in Dostoyevsky's work.

God's answer to our prayer is not a discourse but an action, a passion-filled silence. God answers in the love of His Son. The answer to evil is a figure, a person, a face tormented by suffering that is accepted with love. Zossima becomes another Christ, a wounded healer.

How do we arrive at a new resurrection beyond pain and loneliness? HA Williams [14] uses the image of the late paintings of Vincent Van Gogh. From one point of view what they portray is the horrific and poisonous power of destructive evil. The brush strokes open our eyes to the hell and damnation that lives everywhere - in a field of growing corn, in the sky, in the chairs and tables of a cafe, in the wall of a house, in the features of a friend. Yet it is by means of this horror that Vincent reveals his supreme affirmation of life. For the destructiveness which he portrays does not lead to destruction. The fields of corn, the chairs, the tables, the faces of friends, show no trace of despair. They are aglow with a dark and fierce glory.

Sufferings are part of our lot of being human. In Van Gogh's work the suffering produced paintings aglow with life and vitality. Many of us try to run away from our suffering. Sex, alcohol, social status are some of the things we seek refuge in, only to find that our suffering manages to track us down. The alternative is to accept our suffering as something we must grow through. In our suffering we discover that the self we took as our total self is in fact only a small fraction of what we really are. We begin to discover that there are reserves of compassion and endurance that we did not know we possessed. We also come to face the fact that there are areas in us we do not like so much. We can find an utterly ruthless self-assertion and its by-products, cruelty, callousness, possessiveness, jealousy, envy and hatred. The ultimate challenge of life is to face this capacity for evil and destruction and, by receiving and assimilating it, to transform it into what is positive and creative, so that the dynamic of our evil potential becomes harnessed to what is constructive and good within us. They are like the dark brush strokes of Van Gogh.

It is within this context that we speak of the 'Wounded Healer'. The idea of a wounded healer is to be found in Carl Jung who wrote:

'As a doctor I constantly have to ask myself what kind of message the patient is bringing me. What does he mean to me? If he means nothing, I have no point of attack. The doctor is effective only when he himself is affected. 'Only the wounded physician heals'. But when the doctor wears his personality like a coat of armour, he has no effect. I take my patients seriously. Perhaps I am confronted with a problem just as much as they are. It often happens that the patient is exactly the right plaster for the doctor's sore spot.' [15]

By being in touch with our own pain we can empathise with others in their woundedness. It is tempting to criticise such an attitude by saying that the wounded physician is only exposing his own ugly and festering wound. What must not be forgotten is that the physician in Jung's mind is the one who has worked through his own wounds and comes to a new Easter Day of self-acceptance, healing and compassion.

Jung's words came to have meaning for me. I suffered a number of traumatic events as a young man, had the misfortune to meet with many people who were coldly indifferent and others who hurt me deeply. As a result my wounds remained without healing. However, I had the good fortune to meet John Ryder and Robina Burke, two people filled with love.

They listened to my story with compassion. Their love and empathy were a moment of revelation for me. Their acceptance of me and my story was the beginning of my healing. I am not saying that I have arrived at full healing, but I am on the way. John and Robina have had their own experience of life and through these they have come to accept themselves and use their energies for good. They were wounded healers for me. I found much healing in their compassionate presence. Simone Weil once said, 'God is absent from the world, except for the existence in this world of those in whom his love is alive. Therefore they ought to be present in this world through compassion. Their compassion is the visible presence of God here below.' [16]

Henri Nouwen's work is synonymous with the phrase 'The Wounded Healer' (the title of one of his best known books). These words sum up his ministry of writing and his ministry generally. He was able to be with those who suffer because he knew their pain in his own heart. Nouwen showed that Christ gave the idea of 'Wounded Healer' a fuller interpretation and significance by making his own brokenness the way to liberation and new life. As I argued earlier, he was able to be with those who suffer because he, too, had suffered.

He was brought to new life in resurrection and would be with those who struggle through their suffering to come to a new day, a new resurrection. Likewise ministers who proclaimed liberation and new birth were not called only to care for other people's wounds but to make their own wounds into an important source of healing. They were called to follow Christ and be wounded healers. The wounds Henri Nouwen spoke of were alienation, separation, isolation, and loneliness - these wounds he shared himself and from his wounds he was able to be with others who suffered from the same wounds.

In the 'Wounded Healer', he compares the wound of loneliness to the Grand Canyon - 'a deep incision in the surface of our existence which has become an inexhaustible source of healing and understanding.' [17] The Christian life does not take loneliness away but transforms it into a gift. The painful awareness of loneliness could be an invitation to transcend our limits and work beyond the boundaries of our existence. [18] He goes on to say:

'We ignore what we already know with a deep-seated intuitive knowledge - that no love or friendship, no intimate embrace or tender kiss, no community, commune or collective, no man or woman, will ever be able to satisfy our desire to be released from our lonely condition. This truth is so disconcerting and painful that we are more prone to play games with our fantasies than to face the truth of our existence. Thus we keep hoping that one day we will find the man who really understands our experiences, the woman who will bring peace to our restless life, the job where we can fulfil our potentials, the book which will explain everything, and the place where we can feel at home. Such false hope leads us to make exhausting demands and prepares us for bitterness and dangerous hostility when we start discovering that nobody, and nothing, can live up to our absolutistic expectations.' [19]

A deep understanding of pain makes it possible to convert weakness into strength and to offer experience as a source of healing to those who are lost in the darkness of their own sufferings. Those who offer themselves to others have to walk a tightrope. They should neither conceal their own experience from those they seek to help, nor should they be tempted into any form of spiritual exhibitionism. Open wounds stink and do not heal. [20]

To help the wounded ministers achieve a balance, Nouwen develops the Judaeo-Christian concept of hospitality, seeing it as a place where people allow others to break through their own fears and open themselves to strangers. Hospitality is the ability to pay attention to guests (concentration) and create an empty space where the guests can find themselves and be themselves (community). For Nouwen this is really healing. We can be with others in their pain and be 'wounded healers' to them.

I find Nouwen's book *Compassion*, which he co-wrote with Donald P McNeill and Douglas A Morrison, an important work that shows us how to be wounded healers, to be compassionate with our brothers and sisters. [21] In the first section of the book they consider the compassion of God. We have already looked at this idea in the opening section of this chapter. Jesus reveals God's compassion in his life. He is able to be with those in sorrow or distress because he knows their pain (cf. Heb 2:17-18, 4:14-16). In the section of the compassionate life they show how to get in touch with the compassion of God. They emphasise the importance of discipline and discipleship. [22] Discipline in the Christian life is where we discipline ourselves to allow God's call to reach us and guide us.

It is, however, when we pray that we come in touch with the divine. This requires the discipline of patience. Impatience pulls us away from our prayer. Often people say to themselves 'I'm really too busy to pray' or 'I have so many things to do, I can't get time to myself' or 'Every time I try and pray something comes across my path'. Therefore it requires an honest effort to pray. The discipline of prayer makes us stop and listen, wait and look, trust and see, pay attention and be aware. In prayer we find ourselves in the hands of a compassionate God. Jesus is the wounded healer who shares our pain and his love helps us accept our pain with the hope that we too will come to a resurrection in our lives. It is also in our prayer that we can create a space where our wounded brothers and sisters are welcome and where we bring them and their pain into the hands of the living God. Real prayer brings us closer to our fellow human beings. The intimacy of prayer is the intimacy created by the Holy Spirit who, as the bearer of the new mind and new time, does not exclude but rather includes our fellow human beings. [23] God reveals himself as the one who loves all the members of the human race just as personally and uniquely as he loves us.

Real prayer should lead to some action. When in prayer we come to know the pain of our brothers and sisters, then it also becomes plain that we should actively put into practice the love and compassion we experience in our life with God. The letter of James puts this point succinctly:

'Take the case, my brothers and sisters, of people who have never done a single good act but claims that they have faith. Will that faith save them? If one of the brothers or one of the sisters is in need of clothes and has not enough food to live on, and one of you says to them, 'I wish you well; keep yourself warm and eat plenty' without giving them these bare necessities of life then what good is that? Faith is like that: if good works do not go with it, it is quite dead'. (Jm 2:14-17)

This work brings out the emphasis that fills out the picture of the wounded healer. It is only when we get in touch with God who is all love, that we can begin to accept ourselves and our pain and open ourselves to healing. It is in the strength of this relationship that we can in turn be compassionate with those who are caught in the darkness of grief or depression. We can create a space for them where we can be with them in their pain (hospitality). Compassionate sharing brings healing. It might not bring a total solution for all problems but as I have found in my experience, compassionate and loving sharing of my pain is in its own way a form of healing.

The example of JB Phillips illustrates what Henri Nouwen spoke of. Phillips was an Anglican minister famous for his translations of the Bible. He suffered from depression. His mother died of cancer when he was young and his father pushed him very hard, which left Phillips with a fear of criticism and a longing for praise. As we saw, he believed in an impossible ideal of perfection and tried too hard to live with this impossible ideal. This affected his view of God and his relationship to God. He saw God as an ogre who was demanding the impossible and Phillips saw himself as failing when he did not live up to the demands of this God. He would often remark that those who taught about guilt and judgment made more of an impact than those who preached of God and his love.

His voluminous correspondence gives us insight into the person he was. In a letter to Michael Hollings we get an insight into the darkness of his depression:

'I only know you from the books of prayers which you have compiled with Etta Gullick, and you would know me, if at all, as a translator and Christian writer. Pages 145-6 in your book *The One Who Listens* describe the sort of desolation and darkness which I have tried to endure for something over ten years...

'I can with difficulty endure the days but I frankly dread the nights. The second part of almost every night of my life is shot through with such mental pain, fear and horror that I frequently have to wake myself up in order to restore some sort of balance. If I don't manage to do that it quite often takes me three or four hours after waking to recover anything like a normal attitude towards life.

'My physical health is reasonably good. I have enough of this world's goods for all my needs and am not conscious of any particular unconfessed sins. I have a very wonderful wife who stands by me steadfastly but I cannot help knowing that my almost continuous pain must be a burden to her. It is only during the last few weeks that I have been seriously assaulted by the thought that it isn't worth trying any more, I am too tired to make further effort and I really do not see the slightest ray of hope at the end of this very long tunnel. I think what chiefly worries me, apart from the sense of the loss of God, is the gradual failure of my own powers to love and be concerned about other people. It is true that perfect love casts out fear, but it is revoltingly true that constant fear and tension casts out love. All pain, especially of the mental kind, seems to me to make one more self-centred.

'I don't know whether there is any world of encouragement or hope that you can give me, but since I am told you have had considerable experience with people in the dark places of life I feel it worth asking you.' [24]

Phillips' experience of depression led him into a deep sensitivity for those who were in pain. He was able to be with that person. His letters to a wide variety of people who wrote to him show this. One letter from the many he wrote to helps bear this out. This part of the letter was addressed to a person who was coming to know of God's love but found confession a burden. JB Phillips replied with gentleness and compassion:

'There is a favourite verse of mine which is especially meant for the sensitive and conscientious. It comes in 1 John 3:20 and runs, 'For if our heart condemn us, God is greater than our heart, and knoweth all things'. We may indeed through introspection grow to despise and hate ourselves, but God is greater and more generous than our petty selves and he is far more truly loving and understanding than we ever imagine. You cannot rest too much of your weight upon the real and contemporary God.

I am quite certain that he does not want us to waste any time raking over our sins. He wants us to accept his forgiveness and walk forward confidently in his strength. [25]

Phillips became a wounded healer to many through his writings and letters.

Caryll Houselander

When I think of the idea of 'wounded healer' I also think of Caryll Houselander.

I read her book *The Reed of God* and I was aware of a warm, compassionate human being writing and sharing the quest for faith of her readers.

Caryll died of cancer in London in 1954 at the age of 53 but she accomplished much during that relatively short life. She was a writer, an artist, a poet and a counsellor to many suffering people who came to her seeking her compassion and love. When Caryll was eight or nine she was attacked by a frightening illness that kept her bedridden for three months. The illness came suddenly and Caryll never forgot that time of pain when she suffered in mind as well as in body. She had strong feelings of guilt and scruples. Release from these torments and restored health came when she received Holy Communion, given to her as Holy Viaticum since she was thought to be close to death. This deepened her faith in the sacraments. Her childhood suffering of anxiety neurosis also conditioned her attitude towards those who suffered from psychological suffering. From her own experience she knew what this suffering involved and she was able to be with people who suffered thus. She writes: 'It is largely my experience of these people and their suffering that has confirmed my faith in Christ and in Man, which in a sense is the Catholic Church'. [26]

Before this, however, Caryll had a long journey in faith to make. When Caryll was sixteen her mother asked her to return home from boarding school to what Caryll found to be a curious and puzzling situation. A friend of the family had left a religious order. He was sick in mind and while awaiting an assignment to a parish he had taken refuge at the house of Mrs Houselander, who needed Caryll to assist her in caring for him. Her motives were charitable but tongues began to wag and Caryll found herself ostracised by most of the Catholics she knew, who were scandalized by this arrangement. She came to resent the lack of charity shown to the sick priest by his former Catholic friends, and also noticed the lack of support shown him by his fellow priests.

This was the beginning of Caryll's drift away from the Church. She wrestled with faith and doubt. She had an experience in a church in London which crystallised her growing disenchantment. She went across London in order to get a break from tensions in the house. Unfortunately the church she picked required money from those who sat down to attend mass, and Caryll had not brought any with her. This is her account of what happened.

'I had scarcely knelt down and hidden my face, which was scarlet, when the verger prodded me in the ribs with a collecting bag on the end of a long cane.

'I will go up to the altar of God,' said the priest at the altar.

'To God, the giver of youth and happiness.'

'Sixpence,' said the verger and prodded me again.

I looked up and shook my head.

'Sixpence,' said the verger and went on prodding.

'I haven't got sixpence,' I whispered.

'All right, then,' said the verger, 'you must go into the free seats.'

'There isn't one,' I said.

'Well, then, sixpence.'

I was scalded. There was a priest standing in the aisle watching the scene. When I sprang to my feet and pushed out of the sixpenny seats, he came forward and put his hand on my shoulder.

'You are not going, child?' he said. I shook him off.

'Yes, I am, and I will never come to Mass again.'

I went, beginning the long walk home again, hardly able to stop my tears of rage.

'Thou, O God, art all my strength, why hast Thou cast me off?' said the priest at the altar.

'Why do I go mourning, with enemies pressing me hard?' [27]

However Caryll still longed for a spirituality to guide her life. She went from person to person questioning people about their faith and spirituality. In the end she was guided by religious experiences she had. She had a series of what she called 'visions'. They were certainly seeing for her, though not with the eye of the body but that of the mind. She speaks of them as a 'seeing of the mind' in which the details were known visually. It was through these 'visions' that God began to teach her of the Passion of Christ in men and women, and she was in no doubt that he did it in this way so she could understand.

To understand her visions it is necessary to go back to her experience when she was in school. In her school all the nuns were French, with the exception of a young English woman and a Bavarian lay sister. The Bavarian sister knew little English and her French was limited. So normal communication was difficult for her. The First World War added to her sense of isolation and loneliness, given the strong anti-German sentiment present in England at the time.

One day Caryll passed what was referred to as the boot-room and she saw the Bavarian sister alone cleaning the children's shoes. She stopped and went in to offer to help her. Only when she drew closer could she see the nun was 'weeping soundlessly, tears streaming down her beaten, rosy cheeks. [28] Caryll was embarrassed and just stood there. She tells us: 'At last I looked up and saw that the nun was wearing the Crown of Thorns. It was a great crown, more like a cap of thorns covering her head, and so heavy that it bowed it down.' [29]

Later Caryll was to see that this experience was linked to the second vision she had in July, 1918. This was during the period when she had drifted away from the church. She 'no longer recognised Christ, except in people who were poor and despised, and even in them any recognition was unrealistic'. [30] One rainy London evening she was on her way home when she stopped suddenly in the middle of a drab street. There in front of her was what she could only call a gigantic and living Russian icon. It was an icon of Christ crucified.

Christ was lifted above the world in our drab street, lifted up and filling the sky. His arms reached, it seemed, from one end of the world to the other, the wounds on his hands and feet rubies ... Christ Himself, with His head bowed down by the crown, brooding over the world.' [31]

She learned at the same time of the death of the Tsar. She saw the face of the Tsar in a newspaper and realised that was the same face as the face of Christ that she had seen in the icon. It helped Caryll realise 'that Christ is in kings as well as outcasts, that his passion in the world today is being lived out in kings as well as in common men'. [32]

She was still to experience another 'vision'. This time she came to see Christ living in all people. It occurred while she was travelling during the rush hour in a crowded underground train, a crowded train in which all sorts of people jostled together, sitting and strap-hanging workers of every description going home at the end of the day. 'Quite suddenly I saw with my mind, but as vividly as a wonderful picture, Christ in them all. But I saw more than that; not only was Christ in every one of them, living in them, dying in them, rejoicing in them, sorrowing in them - but because He was in them, and because they were here, the whole world was here too, here in this underground train; not only the world as it was at that moment, not only the people in all the countries of the world, but all those people who had lived in the past, and all those yet to come.

'I came out into the street and walked for a long time in the crowds. It was the same here, on every side, in every passer-by, everywhere - Christ.' [33]

This vision remained with her for a number of days. She began to realise that Christ is in every one.

'Christ is One in all men, as He is One in countless Hosts; everyone is included in Him; there can be no outcasts, no excommunicates, excepting those who excommunicate themselves - and they too may be saved, Christ rising from death in them.' [34]

44

These visions led her to be at peace with the church. During her life the 'vision' would fade but the experience remained a part of her. Her vision of Christ suffering in each individual was strengthened by her prayer. It also formed the basis for the love she bore towards suffering humanity. Her love and compassion brought healing to those who came across her path. A well-known psychologist and neurologist, Dr Eric Strauss, began to send her some of his young patients. He asked her to help by seeing them. Many of them were helped back to health and stability through her love, compassion and empathy. She loved them back to life. Through her experience of illness and visions she had a deep insight into the suffering of others and the presence of Christ in that suffering person. She was a wounded healer.

Before I leave Caryll I would like just to share one last detail from her life. She fell in love with Sidney Reilly, a British spy. Eventually he was captured by the Russians and shot. Even though Caryll was miles away she sensed his suffering and in a mysterious way shared his suffering with him and prayed her love and compassion would reach him. When speaking later to a friend, Charles Scott-Paten, she told him of this. She said she had travelled far, she had been in a prison cell with someone she did not name and she told Charles that she had experienced this person's suffering. She had in some way really seen these events and she had in some inexpressible, inexplicable way really shared his sufferings. [35]

That divine eccentric, Caryll Houselander, would not allow distance or time make her forget her love or stop it from reaching others.

NOTES ON CHAPTER 2

1. P Trible, *God and the Rhetoric of Sexuality* (Philadelphia: Fortress Press, 1978) p31-59
2. CEB Cranfield, *The Gospel According to Saint Mark* (Cambridge: Cambridge University Press, 1994 Edition) p92. See also W. Harrington, *Mark: Realistic Theologian* (Dublin: Columba Press, 1996) p75f.

3. J Marcus, *The Way of the Lord* (Edinburgh: T&T Clark, 1993) p189

4. V Taylor, *The Gospel According to Saint Mark* (London, Macmillan, 1995 Edition) p552

5. HB Swete, *The Gospel According to Saint Mark* (London: Macmillan, 1909) p342

6. HB Swete, op.cit. p342

7. JB Lightfoot, Saint Paul's *Epistle to the Philippians* (London: Macmillan, 1885) p123

8. V Taylor, n(4), p55

9. *The Complete Letters of Vincent Van Gogh* (Greenwich Conn: New York Graphic Society) Vol.1, p197

10. RE Brown, The Death of the Messiah, (London: Chapman, 1994) p227-229

11. B Lindars, *The Theology of the Letter to the Hebrews* (Cambridge: Cambridge University Press, 1991), p44

12. F Dostoyevsky, *The Brothers Karamazov* (Middlesex: Penguin, 1958) p241

13. Cited by P Evdokimov, *Dostoyevsky et le Problème du Mal* (Bruges, Brussels and Paris, 1978) p227

14. H.A. Williams, *True Resurrection* (London: Beazley, 1972) p146

15. C.G. Jung, *Memories, Dreams and Reflections* (London: Fontana Press, 1995 edition) p156

16. Simone Weil, *Writings* selected with an introduction by Eric O Springsted, (New York: Orbis, 1998) p143

17. HJM Nouwen, *The Wounded Healer* (London: Darton, Longman, Todd, 1994 edition) p81-2

18. Ibid, p84

19. Ibid., p84-85

20. Ibid., p88

21. HJM Nouwen, PP McNeill, DA Morrison, 'Compassion', (London:Darton, Longman, Todd, 1999 Edition).

22. Ibid, p89f

23. Ibid p108-9.

24. V Phillips, *The Wounded Healer*, (London: SPCK, 1984), p79-80.

25. V Phillips, op. cit, p71.

26. C Houselander, *A Rocking Horse Catholic* (London: Sheed and Ward, 1987 Edition) p49-50

27. Ibid, p108-109

28. Caryll Houselander, *Born Catholics* (New York: Sheed and Ward 1954) p254

29. Ibid.

30. Ibid, p259

31. C Houselander, *A Rocking Horse Catholic* (London: Sheed and Ward, 1987 Edition), p112

32. C Houselander, *Born Catholics* (New York: Sheed and Ward, 1954), p260

33. C Houselander, A Rocking Horse Catholic', see n (26), p137-138

34. Ibid, p139

35. As quoted by Maisie Ward, *That Divine Eccentric* (London: Sheed and Ward, 1962), p75 In their lifetimes Caryll and Sidney did not marry; why we do not know, but her love remained for him. For further information see RB Lockhart's *Ace of Spies* (New York: Stein and Dary, 1968), p92ff

Also *see*, M. Downey, *Compassion in the New Dictionary of Catholic Spirituality,* p.192f - which I used for background.

CHAPTER 3

JESUS, LONELINESS & SOLITUDE

Jesus Goes to Lonely Places

In Mark 14 we hear of Jesus going from the room of the last supper to Gethsemane to pray. They left for the Mount of Olives singing psalms (14:26). These psalms were possibly the "Hallel" selections from Psalms 114-118 which traditionally ended the Passover meal. On the way Jesus warns the disciples that they will desert him: 'You will all fall away, for the scripture says, I will strike the shepherd and the sheep will be scattered' (14:27). Peter, the first called (1:16-18), protests that even if the others fail he will not. Jesus reaffirms his prediction of Peter's failure but now with a solemn 'amen', saying that he will deny him three times. Peter vehemently rebuts Jesus' prediction saying : 'If I must die with you, I will not deny you.' (14:31). Thus the Jesus who comes to Gethsemane is one who experiences rejection from those he called and trusted. He is the lonely Christ. He is the one who asks Peter, James and John to be with him: "Wait here and stay awake" (14:34c). They sleep and Jesus is left lonelier still.

There were many times in Jesus' life when he felt the need to be apart from others. There were the times he gave himself to prayer. In chapter 1 we read:

'And at once the Spirit drove him out into the wilderness and he remained there for forty days, and was put to the test by Satan. He was with the wild beasts, and the angels looked after him.' (1:12-13)

This happens immediately after the baptism by John in the Jordan. Jesus hears the voice of God telling him: 'You are my son, the beloved, my favour rests on you.' (1:11). The result of Jesus experiencing God was that the spirit drove him out into the wilderness. The voice of God must have disorientated Jesus. It must have left him wondering what his mission was and who he himself was. Mark tells that Jesus was 'driven out' or 'thrown out' (Greek *ekballei*) into the wilderness, in the company of wild beasts and angels. The trials or temptations from Satan test Jesus' insight into the ultimacy of God and his own relation to God. Mark does not tell us the precise nature of these tests. Both Matthew and Luke do. Jesus is offered human rewards to abandon his mission.

Fame and power are dangled before him; he is tempted to prove through the concrete act of throwing himself down from a high place that God really does favour him. He is tempted to manifest his status as beloved of God, thus compromising his mission.

Jesus spends forty days in the wilderness. The forty days and nights allude to Moses and Elijah who wandered for forty days in the wilderness of Sinai and Horeb respectively. (Exodus 24:18 and 1 Kings 19:8). Mark emphasises the forty days Jesus spent in the wilderness rather than emphasising any temptation. Perhaps there was a subtle temptation at work here. Jesus had experienced the closeness of God and the fact that he was loved. I have in mind here a temptation that Carlo Corretto mentions when he spent time in the desert praying and feeling the presence of God [1] He questioned whether he did not hate the company of human beings. His experience of the desert could become an escape. He had to rediscover the needs of human beings. He had to live a life of contemplation amongst his brothers and sisters. Perhaps Jesus felt this way too when he was touched by the presence of God. Yet he too had to leave the desert place and live his life as the beloved of God among people. He brought with him the healing power of God's life into the daily lives of ordinary people. Thus from the very beginning of his ministry Jesus felt the need to go away from engagement in day-to-day living to a place of solitude where he could be with God and then reengage in the affairs of men and women. Solitude here refers to the time and space where a person is alone for the purpose of realising a greater union with God or maintaining a relationship with God.

We next see Jesus praying alone in a quiet place after the first feeding of the crowds. Mark tells us:

'And at once he made his disciples get into the boat and go on ahead to the other side near Bethsaida, while he himself sent the crowd away. After saying goodbye to them he went off into the mountain to pray. When evening came, the boat was far out in the middle of the sea and he was alone on the land. He could see they were distressed in rowing, for the wind was against them; and about the fourth watch of the night he came towards them, walking on the sea. He was going to pass them by, but when they saw him walking on the sea they thought it was a ghost and cried out; for they had all seen him and were terrified. But at once he spoke to them and said "Courage! It's me! Do not be afraid." Then he got into the boat with them and the wind dropped.

They were utterly and completely dumbfounded because they had not seen what the miracle of the loaves meant; their hearts were hardened.' (Mk 6:45-54)

The tumult of a raging sea is a frequent image for confusion and ignorance. Here a deliberate contrast is drawn between Jesus and his disciples, who do not understand either him or what his miracles showed. In the present scene Jesus makes the disciples get into the boat and depart before he dismisses the crowd. They rely on their own devices. Jesus then withdraws to the mountain, alone again in silent prayer. In his relationship with God, which is cultivated in solitude, Jesus becomes renewed and strengthened. He is alone in his prayer. The three passages of Mark that deal with Jesus in prayer (1:35, 6:46 and 14:36, 38) show Jesus praying at night. In 1:35, this is expressly stated, in 6:46 it is suggested by the following section as Jesus meets his disciples 'about the fourth watch of the night' (6:48), and in Gethsemane it is indicated by the fact that the preceding meal with the disciples took place 'when it was evening' (14:18). Night and solitude are the setting for Jesus praying in Mark. Vincent Taylor notes the maxim of Euthymius: 'The mountain, night and solitude are suitable for prayer.'[2]

While night is the time for Jesus' prayerful awareness of the Father, for the disciples darkness signifies their confused, fearful state of mind. Left on their own they have none of the inner strength Jesus had. They did not understand the miracle of the loaves. Jesus has to come and reassure them: 'Courage It's me! Do not be afraid.' (6:50).

In the Gethsemane scene we see Jesus alone and lonely. He asks three of the disciples to be with him (14:33). They sleep and leave Jesus to his fate. As Jesus prays, God is silent. Jesus comes to accept his fate. He comes back to find Peter and the other disciples asleep. He wakes them and tells them this time, to stay awake and pray not to be put to the test (14:38). Mary Ann Tolbert says that we, the audience, should be surprised neither at the disciples' failure to exorcise a demon that requires prayer, nor at their utter incapacity to watch and pray with Jesus in Gethsemane. Prayer in the Gospel of Mark is consistently outside the disciples' range of understanding or participation. [3] Jesus is left alone before the silence of God.

We see this loneliness expressed in the anguished prayer Jesus uttered on the cross: Here Jesus is in extreme need, delivered up to the fury of the ungodly. Here the reference of the prayer is to God and not to his enemies. The Son of Man goes through the lowest depth of human need. The depth is the inferno of dereliction. From this sense of abandonment he cries with full and final force. Prayer finds its extreme expression in the cry of the dying Christ for God - a cry in which a new relationship with God is already intimated.

As Ethelbert Stauffer [4] points out this cry of Jesus does not ring out unheard in cold and empty space. The one who relies on himself and his own power is silenced in his distress. The one who knows that he confronts a divine 'Thou' presses on to God in his distress and brings all his needs before him.

51

The one who also does not know this prayer is overwhelmed by loneliness. Biblical people know a more profound solitariness, namely the abyss of isolation from God. This despairing and mortal loneliness wrings from them the cry in which they say: "Out of the depths, I cry to thee, O God." (Ps 130:1) For a full discussion of the psalms of lament see Chapter 4.

Solitude carries with it the idea of setting aside time and space wherein a person is alone for the purpose of entering into a relationship with God. We see Jesus seeking solitude for prayer. He saw this as integral to building up a communion of love with his Father. This was the heart of Jesus' prayer. Mark showed us such examples of Jesus at prayer in 1:36 and 6:46. In Gethsemane Jesus prays before the silence of God. Here a sense of abandonment and loneliness pervades. Jesus, however, was sustained by his earlier experience of the love of his Father and in the face of God's silence he still trusts and abandons himself into the hands of the One who loved him. We see in Jesus a move from loneliness to solitude wherein he was sustained. We too have to make our journey from loneliness to a solitude where we can be alone with ourselves but sustained by the One who meets us there.

Loneliness

The following is an extract from the diary of Anne Frank:

'Today the sun is shining, the sky is a deep blue, there is a lovely breeze and I am longing - so longing for everything. To talk, for freedom, for friends, to be alone.

'And I do so long ... to cry! I feel as if I am going to burst, and I know that it would be better with crying; but I can't, I'm restless, I go from room to room, breathe through the crack of a closed window, feel my heart beating, as if it is saying, "Can't you satisfy my longing at last?"

'I believe that it is spring within me, I feel that spring is awakening, I feel it in my whole body and soul. It is an effort to behave normally, I feel utterly confused. I don't know what to read, what to write, what to do, I only know that I am longing.' [5]

There is in our hearts a tension, an aching that is non-quietable and deep. Sometimes we feel this ache as centred on a person when we love. Sometimes we feel the ache when we are not accepted and left on the outside. Anne Frank witnesses the loneliness that is often found in our hearts. When we try and spend time alone our ache becomes obvious and we flee silence because the ache seems too painful to bear. We seek escape from loneliness in different ways, for example drink, drugs, sex, but our loneliness refuses to go away and comes back to haunt us.

What are we lonely for? We are lonely for many things:- we are lonely for love and communication. We are lonely for understanding. We are haunted by feelings of insatiability. We want to get to know more people and we want more experiences. We are frustrated because our relationships are fraught with ambiguity, misunderstanding and betrayal. The experience of loneliness can come from alienation, exclusion, rejection, emptiness, frustration and incompleteness. There is something is us that longs for life but at the same time we feel as if we are lost, unable to live the way we crave.

Ron Rolheiser looks at the experience of loneliness and divides it into the following categories. [6] The first is called 'alienation-loneliness', the next is called 'restlessness-loneliness', then 'fantasy-loneliness', 'rootlessness-loneliness' and finally 'blues-loneliness'.

(1) Alienation-loneliness

This refers to the experience of feeling alienated or estranged from others. It is the feeling we have when we are not able to love and understand, and to be loved and understood as fully as we would like to be, or as fully as we should as human beings. Many factors can bring about alienation-

53

loneliness, for example, fear, shame, lack of self-esteem, paranoia, ideological differences with others, selfishness, fear of rejection by others, positive rejection by others, physical or emotional handicaps, physical separation from others, or anything else that hinders us from relating intimately to others as we would like.

Many people can relate to at least one of the above ways of feeling loneliness. Many people are given the feeling that they do not count, or are not valued in any way. It comes to many people in many different ways. It can come to priests, sisters and other religious people. In a way of life that is supposedly centred on the Christ there is often a lack of love and people suffer from the might of such unloving. A life without acceptance is a life in which a most basic need goes unfulfilled; those who feel unaccepted cannot love freely and the darkness of unloving is continued.

There are other examples of alienation-loneliness: the abused child who grows up bitter and resentful and unable to love or accept love; the unattractive boy or girl who is shackled by a negative self-image and whose shame makes it hard for them to reach out. There is the elderly person who is neglected and ignored; the emotionally scarred persons living with a protective shell, unable to venture out. There are the poet-painters - dreamers who are misunderstood and unable to share their depth with others. Here I think of Vincent Van Gogh. In many of these cases the feeling of loneliness can be overwhelming and people often need the care of a compassionate person to share the journey with them in coming to terms with their loneliness.

(2) Restlessness-loneliness

This refers to a feeling of dissatisfaction and restlessness within us which keeps us frustrated and in a state of unrest. Our hearts and minds are so fashioned that they are in some way always unsatisfied, always restless. Religious thinkers have called this 'the spark of the divine with us'. Saint Augustine speaks of his heart being restless and says it will only rest

54

when it comes to rest in God: 'You have made us for yourself, Lord, and our hearts are restless until they rest in you'.[7]

The Greeks have two names for it: *nostos*, a certain homesickness within the human heart, and *eros*, a restless pull towards whatever we perceive as good. The Vikings called it *wanderlust*, the constant urge to explore behind all known horizons.

The Book of Ecclesiastes bears witness to the unsatisfying longing of the human heart in its never-ending search for that which is. He had the courage to say that life is tedious and he is fed up with the pull of pleasure in the world.

'I thought to myself, "Very well, I will try pleasure and see what enjoyment has to offer." And there it was: vanity again! This laughter, I reflected, is a madness, this pleasure no use at all ...

'I did great things: built myself palaces, planted vineyards; made myself gardens and orchards, planting every kind of fruit tree in them. I had pools made for watering the plantations, bought men slaves, women slaves; had home-born slaves as well; herds and flocks I had too, more than anyone in Jerusalem before me. I amassed silver and gold, the treasures of kings and provinces; acquired singing men and singing women and every human luxury ...

'I then reflected on all that my hands had achieved and on all the effort I had put into its achieving. What vanity it all is, and chasing of the wind! There is nothing to be gained under the sun' (Ecclesiastes 2:1-11).

It takes courage to accept and write about such a condition. It can only be said by one who is fully aware that the new reality he is looking for belongs to another dimension, beyond the realities of the world. The tragedy for Qoheleth or Ecclesiastes is that at the time of writing he cannot find where he fits in to the scheme of things and he has not yet entered into a loving relationship with God. His heart is therefore restless. He is no longer happy with the things of this world and he receives less pleasure from things as time goes by. He has to move on. This is how he speaks of the days of this world which are passing away:

55

'Light is sweet; at sight of the sun the eyes are glad. However great the number of the years a man may live, let him enjoy them all, and yet remember that dark days will be many. All that is to come is vanity.

'Rejoice in your youth, you who are young; let your heart give you joy in your young days. Follow the promptings of your heart and the desires of your eyes.

'But this you must know; for all these things God will bring you to judgment.

'Cast worry from your heart, shield your flesh from pain.

'Yet youth, the age of dark hair, is vanity. And remember your creator in the days of your youth, before evil days come and the years approach when you say, "These give me no pleasure", before sun and light and moon and stars grow dark, and the clouds return after the rain; the day when those who keep the house tremble and strong men are bowed; when the women grind no longer at the mill, because day is darkening at the windows and the street doors are shut; when the sound of the mill is faint, when the voice of the bird is silenced, and song notes are stilled, when to go uphill is an ordeal and walk is something to dread.

'Yet the almond tree is in flower, the grasshopper is heavy with food, and the caper bush bears its fruit, while man goes to his everlasting home. And the mourners are already walking to and fro in the street before the silver cord has snapped, or the golden lamp been broken, or the pitcher shattered at the spring, or the pulley cracked at the well, or before the dust returns to the earth as it once came from it, and the breath to God who gave it.

'Vanity of vanities, Qoheleth says. All is vanity' (Ecclesiastes 11:7-12, 8).

(3) Fantasy-loneliness

This is the loneliness caused by our failure to be completely in contact with truth, reality as it is in itself. Theologians such as Thomas Aquinas believe that we attain truth, and live in truth, when our thoughts correspond to the way reality is in itself. Conversely when there is a discrepancy between the two - mind and reality - we suffer illusion, fantasy or error.

The image of one who sees a mirage in the desert shows us the difference between illusion and reality.

All of us, to some degree, live in fantasy and illusion. Many of us daydream about achieving something and we can get our fantasies mixed in the way we perceive reality. The degree that we are not truly in touch with reality is a measure of our alienation and loneliness.

In our minds we can see ourselves as an 'intellectual', 'a mystic', 'a nice person to know' or many other things. We might be in some degree any of the above, but there is also the shadier side of our personality. When we are weak, when we can let ourselves and others down then the pain of our reality can be hard to take. Life can and does unmask many of our illusions.

Fantasy-loneliness can be understood by its most extreme forms. For instance a psychotic person can be so out of touch with reality that he or she can imagine themselves to be some important figure from the past, such as Jesus, or Napoleon. Somebody taking mind-altering drugs can imagine they are undergoing mystical experiences. There is, in these cases, a discrepancy between the person's state of mind and reality. The people above are divorced from reality. They are losing contact with God, with reality and with others. They are slipping into imprisonment within the lonely confines of their own mind.

(4)   Rootlessness-loneliness

This is the type of loneliness we feel when we experience ourselves without roots, without anchors, without a place where we can feel secure, and lacking something which would anchor us with the flow of time. Some people experience life as a storm, constantly changing and in flux. To feel safe from the storm, watching it indoors, is different from being caught in the storm. Many of the things that used to give security such as family ties, family values, unshakeable truths and trusted institutions, are constantly being questioned, examined and shaken from the secure place they used to occupy in the past. People can cry out for some place to shelter, some place to feel secure. The mood and events of our times militate against finding such security. Abuse of children by trusted priests and religious has shaken the faith of a great many people who once found the church a safe refuge. 'Is there anything we can believe in?' some ask. In society too much of what we believed of people in the past is being debunked

Our heroes are seen to walk with feet of clay. Many of the moral values of the past are questioned in magazines, radio and TV chat-shows. All around us is insecurity. This type of loneliness is exemplified by the young people who claim to have received everything from their parents, except something to believe in.

Ron Rolheiser narrates a story about Teilhard de Chardin.[8] He tells how at the age of five when he was getting a haircut, the young Teilhard was fascinated by the way his hair shrivelled up and was burnt in the fire. He was filled with sadness at the passing away of such things. A few days later he collected some pieces of iron because he believed they would not disappear but he found that they too rusted and decayed. Then he tried collecting rocks to see if they would last. Teilhard did this when he was five years of age. Later, as an adult, his mind would attempt to seize upon truths that were indestructible, capable of withstanding the ravages of fire and rust, whim and fashion, relativity and contingency.

(5) Blues-loneliness

This type of loneliness is experienced on a random or sporadic basis. Blues-loneliness is really a form of psychological depression which people call simply 'loneliness'. It is a pulse of loneliness which may be short-lived, causing intense pain at the time. For those who suffer from depression this feeling of loneliness can be of longer duration and this

58

loneliness can colour the whole way we see things. This is the kind of loneliness I experience in my depression and it blocks my capacity to share in life.

Blues-loneliness in itself may be caused by a combination of the other types of loneliness, with additional depression and nostalgia. Other events can trigger the feeling of the blues in us. These events can range from the season of the year to the season of our life, to the death of a loved one. We hear tell of 'getting over a death' or 'mid-life crisis'. For most people these do not constitute insurmountable obstacles but are stages people work through to come to new life. Those who suffer clinical depression find this pain to be long-lasting and deeper.

We saw Jesus driven by the spirit to go into the wilderness or desert (Mk 1:12-13). The spirit drives us into the true wilderness which is ourselves in our isolation and pain. Just as Jesus met God in a lonely place so our wilderness experiences open up for us the lonely place where we too can meet God and come to new life. However it is not as simple as that because in our loneliness we can be tempted to despair, to turn to cynicism and be tempted to turn away from those we love, asking 'what's the use?' We can be tempted to banish love from our lives because it costs too much and we are in too much pain. Yet in all this, Christ is there to meet us in our wilderness. As we see in Mark's compassionate Jesus, he does not withdraw his love from us. In our loneliness one can begin to take faltering steps to come to meet him in solitude.

Solitude

Henri Nouwen wrote about loneliness. He described loneliness as one of the most universal sources of human suffering today. [9] Psychiatrists and psychologists speak about it as the most frequently expressed complaint and the root not only of an increasing number of suicides but also of alcoholism, drug use and different psychosomatic symptoms such as headaches, low back pain and stomach-aches and ulcers.

The roots of loneliness are very deep and cannot be touched by optimistic advertisement, substitute love image or social togetherness. Loneliness has its roots in the suspicion that there is no-one who cares and offers love without conditions and no place where we can be vulnerable without being used.

Nouwen says in another place: 'One way to express the spiritual crisis of our time is to say that most of us have an address but cannot be found there' [10] We are not at home with ourselves and people for the time when we feel our loneliness.

Solitude refers to the time and space wherein a person is alone for the purpose of realising union with God. The example of Jesus seeking solitude for prayer shows the way we should move in our personal journey. However, the feeling of loneliness hinders us from entering solitude. The experience of not being accepted, of hurt, and the feeling that we are not of much value causes us to run away from being alone. We come to feel our own pain and to doubt that we can be loved by anyone, even God. Entering a private room and shutting the door does not mean that we shut out our inner doubts, anxieties, fears, bad memories, unresolved conflicts, angry feelings, all impulsive desires. Often these come more to the fore and we can be tempted to despair at the sense of our own weakness. This is where the spiritual discipline of our lives comes into play.

Jesus was driven to lonely places to pray and here he realised union with God. He too had his experience of loneliness in Gethsemane but he shared his pain with God who appeared silent and came to unite his will with God's.

Henri Nouwen says that 'when we are not afraid to enter our own centre and to concentrate on the stirrings of our own soul, we come to know that being alive means being loved'. [11] The experience tells us that we can only love because we are born out of love. The compassionate Jesus who felt loneliness, rejection and the temptation to give up is the one who meets us in our loneliness. And with him we become less afraid to be alone. In the midst of pain we can meet God. Jesus reveals

60

to us the compassion of God. It is with him that we can begin the journey from loneliness to solitude, the journey to coming to know that we are, in spite of appearance, held by God who loves us.

Catherine De Hueck Doherty narrated such a journey from loneliness to solitude. [12] She had been to see a film on Nicholas and Alexandra and after the film was filled with a sense of loneliness. Memories of her homeland once again came flooding back to her. She goes on to say:

'But the realisation that was overwhelming me most of all - like a sea in which I was drowning, now surfacing, now overcome by it again, the overwhelming wave of remembrance tonight was that I was a stranger in a strange land. There was no denying it. I lived with values different from other people's. I was beginning to understand more deeply the darkness of which Saint John of the Cross and Saint Teresa of Avila speak. In such a darkness there is only one light and that light is God. Unless you hold on to him, you become enmeshed in the meshes of the devil. For the first time since I have started coming to my poustinia, I knew that I was being tempted by self-pity. I also knew that the temptation was well directed because ever since I came to Canada I have been lonely, lonely with a cosmic loneliness of a refugee whom nobody understands or wishes to, and who perhaps was only understood after a long and arduous fight.' [13]

Catherine was overcome with the feeling of loneliness, of not belonging, of being a stranger in a strange land. She realized that this loneliness had been with her for a long time and now it was coming to the surface and she found herself lonely and depressed. In this state she withdrew to her *poustinia.* Put, very simply, this was a place of solitude where she could be alone with God. Here a new realisation came to her. 'That was my true vocation - and I never understood it! I did not understand that it was the vocation of loneliness, that God had invited me to share his loneliness because this was to be the vocation of many. Many people don't realise that their loneliness is an invitation to share the loneliness of God.' [14]

She saw that God had asked her to share in the moment of Gethsemane. This enabled her to share the pain of others who came across her path. She was a wounded healer who exercised a ministry of compassion. She had moved from loneliness to solitude.

A Friend on the Journey:

Bernard Bro [15] speaks of the people of our age confronting loneliness and the desperate quest for a meaning in life. Each individual searches for authentic existence and true life. He cites the following texts as exemplifying this quest to come to terms with our loneliness.

'There's my old pain again, down in the pit of my stomach, like an ulcer, hurting whenever I move. I know what it's called. Its name is fear of being alone for ever. And to this, I fear, there is no answer.' (Camus)

'I prayed, I pleaded for a sign, I sent Heaven messages: no reply. Heaven doesn't even know my name. I kept wondering what I was in God's eyes. Now I know the answer: nothing. God doesn't see me, God doesn't hear me, God doesn't know me. You see the void above our heads? That is God. You see this hole in the ground? That's what God is. You see this crack in the door? That's God too. Silence is God. Absence is God. God is human loneliness.' (Sartre).

Camus and Sartre express here the deep loneliness of our age. Sartre speaks of God not knowing us and being silent before our tears. Camus speaks of the ache of the human heart. To these two authors Bro added this:

'When, exhausted by the darkness surrounding me, I try to refresh my heart with the memory of the luminous country to which I aspire, my torment grows twice as great. Borrowing sinners' voices, the darkness seems to mock me, saying: "You dream of light, of a homeland redolent with sweetest perfumes, you dream of eternally possessing the Creator of all these marvels, you believe that one day you'll emerge from the surrounding fog! Keep going! Keep going! Look forward to death but it will not give you what you hope for - only deeper darkness than ever, the darkness of extinction." '

I was amazed to find that these words came from St. Thérèse of Lisieux.(d.1897) I had often heard of her little ways, her giving of herself in the daily routine of her life, her self-sacrifice in the ordinary things. The words expressed here moved me deeply. I could hear the voice of my own doubts and loneliness expressed in a way I did not have the courage to express.

At the age of fifteen Thérèse made her decision to enter the Carmel Monastery in Lisieux. She thought she had prepared herself fairly well for what was to come. She was under no illusion about what was ahead of her in terms of the austerity of the life and the reaction the nuns would have towards her. At Carmel she got used to early rising, long hours in chapel, poor food, inadequate heating, a small cell with a straw mattress. She would spend most of the day in silence and do manual work.

The first shock she got when she entered the monastery was the mental illness that afflicted her father. He was the one Thérèse adored and the one who radiated love and compassion. She could see God's love and compassion reflected in her father and now he had to bear the cross of mental illness. As the illness grew worse her world was shattered and it would take much prayer and pondering before she came to terms with the sadness of her father's fate.

In her time in Carmel she began to wonder where her true vocation lay. She wanted to be a priest, a warrior. She desired many things. She describes in her own words how she came to find her true calling:

'To be a martyr was the dream of my youth. And in the cloisters of Carmel the dream grew with me. But even then I realised that dream was absurd, because I couldn't limit my desires to a specific kind of martyrdom ... I opened St Paul's epistles in the hopes of finding an answer. My eye chanced to fall on the 12th and 13th chapters of the First Epistle to the

Corinthians. There I first read that not all can be apostles, prophets, doctors, etc ... This answer did not satisfy my desires ... I read on ... and the Apostle explains how all the most perfect gifts are nothing without Love ... At last I had found peace ... I realised that Love covered every type of vocation, that Love was everything, that it embraced all times and places ... Then, in the excess of my delirious joy, I exclaimed: Love is my vocation!' [16]

Thérèse's vocation would prove a challenge to many. Love was the heart of her vocation and should be the heart of the church and its individual members. Love is found to be lacking in some church people and other people carry within their spirits the wounds of such unloving.

She offered herself in total love to the Father. Her offering stresses a vision of her offering as a martyrdom, a sense of her offering being renewed through her life and into eternity. [17] The following is the text of her offering of herself in love:

In order to live in one single act of perfect Love, *I offer myself as a victim of holocaust to your merciful love*, asking You to consume me incessantly, allowing the waves of infinite tenderness shut up within You to overflow into my soul, and that thus I may become a martyr of Your Love, O my God! May this martyrdom, after having prepared me to appear before You, finally cause me to die and may my soul take its flight without any delay into the eternal embrace of Your Merciful Love. I want, O my Beloved, at each beat of my heart to renew this offering to You an infinite number of times, until the shadows having disappeared I may be able to tell You of my Love in an Eternal face to Face!'

Her desire 'to live in one single act of perfect love' corresponds with her desire to love God and make him loved. She was to live this offering of love in a radical way in the last eighteen months of her life. On Good Friday, 1896, she had her first haemoptysis which was an early sign of the tuberculosis that was to ravage her body. She also fell into a deep darkness where she came to doubt all that she believed before. It was in this state that she was tempted to take her life. It was here she expressed her temptation to doubt. However, in the midst of her loneliness she continued to hope against hope and remain loyal to her vocation of love in spite of the darkness that she found herself in. She spoke thus:

'Lord, your child has understood your divine light; she asks pardon for her brothers, she consents to eat for as long as you wish it the bread of sorrow, and she will not rise from this table, which is filled with bitterness, where poor sinners eat, until the day you have appointed. Further, can she not say in their name, in the name of her brothers, "Have pity on us, Lord, for we are poor sinners"? I told him that I am happy not to enjoy heaven on earth in order that he may open heaven for ever to poor unbelievers.' [18]

Thérèse identifies with her brothers and sisters who are caught up in their world of loneliness and   alienation. She knows in her heart the pain of those who are tempted to unbelief and those tempted to despair. Her knowledge of these things comes from her own heart where she experienced these things. She makes her acts of faith, hope and love on behalf of her brothers and sisters because she is precisely where they are. All that is left for her after all consolation is gone is the desolate cry 'I thirst!' ('J'ai soif!')

Her whole being was one of prayer offered to the Father in the company of those who felt lonely and far away from God. She expressed a total love of God and a total belief in God in the very predicament where many people find themselves. This is the secret of Thérèse's appeal for me. She expresses her sense of loss and loneliness in her prayer. She reflects the lonely Jesus in Gethsemane. Through her prayer she shows herself a sister to those who are lonely, and walks with us on our journey to God. She introduces us to the lonely Christ, shows us that as doubters and lonely people, we are welcome in the eyes of God.

Notes on Chapter 3

1. C Carretto, *In Search of the Beyond* (Tiptree, Essex: Darton, Longman and Todd: 1966) p115f.

2. V Taylor, *The Gospel According to St Mark* (London: Macmillan: 1995 edition) p328.

3. MA Tolbert, *Sowing the Gospel* (Minneapolis: Fortress Press: 1989) p189.

4. E Stauffer, Boaõ, in TDNTI, p628.

5. Anne Frank, *The Diary of Anne Frank* (N.Y: Doubleday, 1959)

6. R Rolheiser, *The Restless Heart* (London: Spire, 1990 edition) P.61-81.

7. St Augustine, *Confessions* Book 1, Chapter 1.

8. R Rolheiser, see n(6), p77.

9. Henri JM Nouwen, *Reaching Out* (Glasgow: Collins, Son: 1976) P.26f.

10. Henri JM Nouwen, *Seeds of Hope: A Henri Nouwen Reader* (London: DLT, 1998) p60

11. Henri JM Nouwen, *The Wounded Healer in Ministry and Spirituality* (New York: Dayspring: 1998) p164.

12. Catherine De Hueck Doherty, *Poustinia* (Glasgow: Collins. 1975) p202-205.

13. Catherine De Hueck Doherty, op. cit, p202-203.

14. ibid, p204.

15. B Bro, *The Little Way* (London; Darton, Longman, Todd.1979) p54f.

16. B Bro, op. cit, p5-6

17. Christopher O'Donnell, *Love in the Heart of the Church* (Dublin: Veritas 1997) p41.

18. As quoted by Simon Tugwell, *Ways of Imperfection* (London. Darton, Longman, Todd. 1984) p227-228.

CHAPTER 4
THE PRAYER OF LAMENT AND JESUS

Jesus says to his disciples: "I am deeply grieved even unto death: remain here and keep awake." (14:34) With stunning boldness Mark presents Jesus as engulfed in the prayer of lament. He is in line with the tradition of the just ones of Israel - anguished before death, tormented by the betrayal of friends, vulnerable to enemies. Jesus clings to the one who gives meaning to his existence, the God of Israel. The motif of betrayal by friends was part of a Jewish tradition reflecting on the sufferings of the just one, who is abandoned and tormented, his only hope being God's fidelity. This Old Testament motif has influenced the Synoptic passion traditions. [1] The present scene places us in the context of faith in the one who appears silent.

In the Psalms we hear the echo of the just one in agony. Many of these psalms have verbal echoes in the Gethsemane scenes:

'To thee, O Lord, I cried;
And to the Lord I made supplication
"What profit is there in my death,
if I go down to the Pit?
Will the dust praise thee?
Will it tell of they faithfulness?
O Hear, O Lord, and be gracious to me!
O Lord, be thou my helper!" ' (Ps 30:8-10)

'Do not thou, O Lord, withhold
They mercy from me,
Let thy steadfast love and thy faithfulness

Ever preserve me!
For evils have encompassed me
Without number
My iniquities have overtaken me,
Till I cannot see;
They are more then the hairs of my head
My heart fails me.' (Ps 40:11-13)

'I say to God, my rock:
"Why has thou forgotten me?
Why go I mourning?
Because of the oppression of the enemy?"
As with a deadly wound in my body,
My adversaries taunt me,
While they say to me continually,
"Where is your God?"
Why are you cast down, O my soul,
And why are you so diquieted
Within me?' (Ps 42:9-11)

'Vindicate me, O God, and
Defend my cause against an ungodly people;
From deceitful and unjust men
Deliver me!
For thou art the God in whom I take refuge;
Why hast thou cast me off?
Why go I mourning
Because of the oppression of my enemy?

Why are you cast down, O my soul,
And why are you so disquieted
Within me?' (Ps 43:1-2,5)

'My heart is in anguish within me,
The terrors of death have fallen
Upon me.
Fear and trembling come upon me,

And I say, "O that I had wings like
A Dove!
I would fly away and be at rest;
Yet, I would wander afar,
I would lodge in the wilderness,
I would hast to find me a shelter
From the raging wind and tempest." ' (Ps 55:4-8)

'Hear my cry, O God,
Listen to my prayer;
From the end of the earth I call to thee,
When my heart is faint.

Lead thou me
To the rock that is higher than I;
For thou art my refuge,
A strong tower against the enemy.' (Ps 61:1-3)

The snares of death encompassed me;
The pangs of Sheol laid hold on me;
I suffered distress and anguish.
Then I called on the name of the Lord:
"O Lord, I beseech thee, save
my life!" ' (Ps 116:3-4)

Donald Senior [2] thinks it unlikely that Mark (or the tradition before him) relied directly on any specific psalm text. The lament prayer was a well-known and classic prayer of the Hebrew scriptures. The passion tradition in the New Testament is the sole place in the New Testament where this type of prayer is retained. [3]

The intensity of Jesus' anguish is directly stated in v.34: 'I am deeply grieved, even to death.' The phrase 'deeply grieved' or 'deeply sorrowful' repeats the ideas found in the laments of Ps 42:6, 11 and 43:5. One also thinks of the prophet Elijah who was depressed and dejected after his treatment by Jezebel and the rejection he encountered (1 Kg 19:18), and also of the prophet Jonah (4:9). There is no hint in the text of Mark that Jesus' distress is caused by an awareness of the sins of the world. Such pious reflection blunts the force of Mark's narrative. The evangelist presents Jesus as an example of brilliant faith, a tormented child of God in love with life and fearful of death, without support except for his faith in God's fidelity. He asks Peter, James and John to remain with him and stay awake, but they sleep. So the anguish of Jesus is compounded.

Jesus separates himself a short distance from the three disciples and as a further sign of the intensity of his anguish he casts himself on the ground in prayer. Jesus, who has expended his energy in healing broken bodies and minds, in casting out demons, who had raised Jairus' daughter from the grip of death, now finds himself about to have his body broken and his spirit caught in the vice of ultimate evil. And so he prays for deliverance, as believers had done before in the laments of Israel. This opens the door for us to explore the psalms of lament.

Healing Power of the Psalms

(a) The Psalms in general

The psalms were the prayers of the Jewish community offered in the temple. The idea of temple is important here. Among the Romans *templum* was a space in the sky or on the earth sectioned off for the augurs to read the omens. It came, therefore, to refer to a sacred space, marked off from other space, where the augurs would examine the entrails of birds. Thus the temple was the place where sacred persons looked at the 'insides of things' (animals) to discover divine meanings and purposes. From this we derive the world 'temple', a sacred place where people go to meet God, and thus to communicate with God and seek to know His purpose. The word contemplation also has its roots here.

The psalms were the prayers the Jews uttered when they entered this sacred space. James Mays has called the psalms the liturgy of the kingdom of God. He writes: '... the words of the psalms are the vocabulary of a particular language world. We must, by means of the psalms, enter and live in that language world if praise and prayer with their words are to be authentic.' [4]

When we pray the psalms we enter a world in which God reigns. Mays goes on to express this insight in the following words:

'I am using the somewhat opaque term "language world" to avoid the implication that what is at issue is a language in the general sense, like classical Hebrew or Hellenistic Greek. What is at issue is not simply grammar, syntax and vocabulary, but an interrelated set of sentences that comprise a semantic sphere and the particular understanding and rendering of "world" and "existence" expressed in them ... The coherence and reference of the pslamic language world is based on a sentence on which all that is said in the psalms depends. Everything else is connected to what this one sentence says. It is a liturgical cry that is both a declaration of faith and a statement about reality. In Hebrew the sentence is composed of only two words: the proper name of Israel's god and the way for becoming, being and acting as a sovereign. The sentence is "*Yhwh malak*", "the Lord reigns". Whatever else is said in the psalms about God and God's way with the world and human beings is rooted in the meaning and truth of this metaphor. It is systemic for psalmic language.' [5]

Many claim that for a community of faith to properly use the psalms, they must reinterpret their entire world in the light of the language world of the psalms. 'The Lord reigns' (*Yhwh malak*) is the crucial part of allegiance and statement of faith and life. God and world and human life are understood in terms of the reign of the Lord. [6]

'...When you read or recite the psalms, when you pray and praise through them, you are set in the midst of this language world and led to speak of reality as it does. You are invited and instructed to experience and understand world and self, society and history, through the linguistic prism of a theological sovereignty shaped by the character of a particular god.

'The dissonance of this language with the one taught by our culture, its incongruity with the sensibility of modernity, is apparent ... It centres on a sovereign god instead of a sovereign self' [7]

Language creates worlds. So, to inhabit a language is to inhabit a whole world. Ludwig Wittgenstein put forward this idea when he said: '...to imagine a language means to imagine a form of life.' [8] The world we inhabit when we pray the psalms is a world where God reigns and where we try to make sense out of our human experience. It is also where we talk about God and to God.

Dermot Cox says that the world of the psalms is where God seeks human beings. [9] God takes the initiative, and it is His word that creates the hearer's reply. The positive and negative features that mark such psalms at 30 and 119 represent the real crisis that is inherent in such dialogue, for it presents a God who offers Himself and who may be refused. Acceptance or rejection of a divine initiative is always there as an option. Biblical prayer cannot be divorced from concrete response to a personal experience of encounter with God. This response is actualised in the psalm.

Ps 95 ends with a warning that is as real to first century Israel as it was centuries earlier at Sinai: 'O that today you would listen to his voice.' The 'today' of this challenge is as real a moment of crisis for every successive generation in Israel as the Sinai experience had been for Moses and his community. This is in fact the function of V.7 as it stands in the text:

"For he is our God,
And we are the people of his pasture,
And the sheep of his land.
O that today you would listen to his voice." (Ps 95.7)

The first part of this verse contains the recitation of the covenant formula in poetic form (he is our God, we the people of his pasture). This forms the motivation for the response of the community (vv 8-11) to the divine encounter that marked the first part of the psalm. God presents himself in an act of deliverance and the believer responds in praise.

Similarly, in suffering the individual raises a lament (secure in the historical perception of Yahweh) and God intervenes to save. The frequent joy of the psalmist is a response to the encounter with God. Thus the psalms can be seen as a form of dialogue with the divinity who always makes himself present. One comes into the presence of God in these prayers. The psalms become an arena of encounter with God. They show us God wishes to meet us in our humanity and the way we are. The psalms also show us how to respond to this encounter. In the psalms God reveals himself to the one who prays. The psalms inaugurate a relationship with a known person (God) and this takes place within the categories of the psalms. The psalms are dominated by a dialogue structure. We have a divine intervention (of redemption and creation) and a human reaction.

The psalms represent a personal search for God. They seek to find a meaning for the one who prays in the light of God's revelation in the past. Ps 27 contains the following verse:

'When evildoers assail me,
Uttering slanders against me,
My adversaries and foes,
They shall stumble and fall.
Though a host encamp against me,
My heart shall not fear;
Though war arise against me,
Yet I will be confident.' (Ps 27, 2-3)

The psalmist relives, now, an experience that happened in the past. It is where the psalmist comes to encounter God and find meaning in his present state. It enables him to start afresh.

The God who acted in this way in the past is the God the psalmist meets now. Just as he looked after his people in the past so now he is present and will hear the prayer of the psalmist.

Dermot Cox [10] uses the idea of sacrament to help us see God's coming to us in the psalms. He explains that God's self-revelation in the Old-Testament is a progressive series of interactions in time that thrusts towards an eschatological terminus, and Israel celebrates liturgical events in which the great events of the past are recalled in the present. We see an example of this in Joshua 24 after the first generation had died out in the wilderness along with Moses. Yet this new audience took on the implications of the covenant just as their ancestors had done:

'Then Joshua gathered all the tribes of Israel to Shechem, and summoned the Elders, the heads, the judges, and the officers of Israel; and they presented themselves before God. And Joshua said to all the people, "Thus says the Lord, the God of Israel, "Your fathers lived of old beyond the Euphrates, Terah, the father of Abraham and of Nahor; and they served other gods ..."

'Now therefore fear the Lord, and serve him in sincerity and in faithfulness; put away the gods whom your fathers served beyond the River, and in Egypt, and serve the Lord. And if you be unwilling to serve the Lord, choose this day whom you will serve, whether the gods your fathers served in the region beyond the river, or the gods of the Amorities in whose land you dwell; but as for me and my house, we will serve the Lord.'

The Israelites are to choose 'this day' the obligations of the covenant. God's past deeds are made present again in the words of Joshua and the people are asked to respond 'this day' to God's saving deeds. Deuteronomy 5:3 and 26:5-9 also re-echo this theme. The Sinai covenant is real for the readers. We participate in the historical situations now, today; 'and behold, now, I bring the first fruit of the ground, which you, O Lord, have given me.' (Deut. 26:10).

This helps us to see the way of Christ and how he met God in his prayer. The psalm inserted the reader into the reality of a divine act of liberation, which was made present again, today,

74

in the words of the psalm.. This, Cox terms a form of sacrament. Ps100 functions in the same way as Joshua 24 and Deuteronomy. In v.2 we hear the phrase "... come into his presence ... with singing". God was thought of as being actually there, his presence evoked by the act of singing or recital. This had been guaranteed by the events of Sinai. This same God was the one present to the psalmist and those who prayed the psalm. Later on in the psalm we are invited to meet God, who is present, and come before his face:

'Know that the Lord is God!
It is he that made us, and we are his;
We are his people, and the sheep of his pasture.
Enter his gates with thanksgiving,
And his courts with praise!
Give thanks to him, bless his name!'

Through the act of recitation of the psalm this presence of God exercises its influence. Ps 81 clearly suggests this:

'Sing aloud to God our strength;
Shout for joy to the God of Jacob!
Raise a song, sound the timbrel, the sweet lyre with the
harp.
Blow the trumpet at the new moon, at the full moon, on our
feast day.
For it is a statute for Israel, an ordinance of the God of
Jacob.
He made it a decree in Joseph, when he went out over the
land of Egypt.

I hear a voice I had not known:
"I relieved your shoulder of the burden;
your hands were freed from the basket.
In distress you called, and I delivered you;
I answered you in the secret place of thunder;
I tested you at the waters of Meribah." '

The voice that the psalmist heard but did not know (V.5-c) is that of God and forms a bridge to V.6-16. The first five verses constitute a call to prayer and the rest of the psalm is the result of that invitation. We hear Yahweh say to those reciting the psalm: '... in distress you call and Yahweh delivered you.' Those who pray the psalm share in the past saving events of Yahweh in history even now, today. The one who prays the psalms is 'now' challenged by the Meribah event (V.6, 7a,b). The rest of the psalm reiterates the need for a personal response (V.8-9) based on the effectiveness of the historical Exodus event now present to the hearer: 'I am the Lord your God who brought you out of the land of Egypt. Open your mouth wide and I will fill it.' (V.10). The cultic recital of the psalm becomes a sacrament of encounter, remembrance of the past deeds of liberation in the Exodus from Egypt effecting the insertion of the hearer into the reality of that saving event. Worship is not merely the result of religious experience. It also creates it anew, so that an experience such as that of the Red Sea deliverance or the Sinai covenant becomes each worshipper's experience. This was the world those who prayed the psalms experienced. Jesus belonged to this line.

(b) The Psalms and Human Emotions

Human needs take many forms. People can find themselves depressed, rejected and very much alone in a world in which they perceive God as inactive and divorced from our world of pain. People can lose meaning for themselves and for this life. The figures for suicide indicate this. The people of the Old Testament used prayer to help them come to terms with their pain. Ps 17:1-3 expresses faith that God is present when one prays:

'Hear a just cause, O Lord;
Attend to my cry!
Give ear to my prayer from lips free of deceit!
From thee let my vindication come!

Let thy eyes see the right!
If thou tryest my heart, if thou visitest me by night,
If thou testest me, thou wilt find no wickedness in me:
My mouth does not transgress.'

This is formally a 'lament'. In this type of psalm it can be seen that sickness, pain, loneliness, depression or any burden that one carries can become an arena in which one meets God and rediscovers the peace, the *shalom*, that comes from being with God.

In Ps 12:5 we have affirmed for us the effectiveness of our prayer and that God hears us:

' "Because the poor are despoiled,
because the needy groan,
I will now arise," says the Lord;
"I will place him in the safety for which he longs." '

Ps 55:16 expresses the faith of the psalmist that his prayer is heard:

'But I call upon God;
and the Lord will save me.'

The psalmist believed that there does come a moment of change when an oppressive situation is reversed and one comes to know God anew and feel his presence. For those who suffer this moment might seem like just a dream with no substance in reality and that one ends up as before, feeling lonelier still. It is good to go on this journey through the psalms of lament, a path which Jesus trod, and attempt to make an act of faith with the psalmist, to hope against hope.

Every lament, according to Dermot Cox is a spiritual replay of Ex.2:23-25:[11]

'In the course of those many days the King of Egypt died. And the people of Israel groaned under their bondage, and cried out for help, and their cry under bondage came up to God. And God heard their groaning, and God remembered his covenant with Abraham, with Isaac, and with Jacob. And God saw the people of Israel, and God knew their condition.'

In the lament emphasis is placed on the act of faith and confidence, that is the point of making present the historical events of the past. The act of faith is in God hearing the prayer of the one who calls like Israelites of old.

Ps 86 is an individual lament. It is the cry of one who is lost and alienated. It is the prayer of one who does not hear God, but only finds that He is apparently silent. It is precisely by praying through this silence that the psalmist reaches out to find God:

'Thou art my God; be gracious to me, O Lord,
For to thee do I cry all the day.
Gladden the soul of thy servant,
For to thee, O Lord, do I lift up my soul.
For thou, O Lord, art good and forgiving,
Abounding in steadfast love to all who call on thee.
Give ear, O Lord, to my prayer;
Hearken to my cry of supplication.
In the day of my trouble I call on thee,
For thou dost answer me.' (v.2b-7)

The psalmist believes that by reaching out thus God has in some way entered the situation, however obscure this encounter might appear. No other answer is deemed necessary:

'I give thanks to thee, O Lord my God,
With my whole heart,
And I will glorify thy name forever.' (v.12)

In Psalm 6 we do not know what has brought the psalmist to lament, but we do recognise his need of meeting God. In v.4 we hear the psalmist say, 'Lord, O Lord, save my life; deliver me for the sake of your steadfast love.' The psalmist needs to meet and come into a relationship with him. This throws light on the opening verses of the psalm:

'O Lord, rebuke me not in thy anger,
Nor chasten me in thy wrath.
Be gracious to me, O Lord, for I am languishing;
O Lord, heal me, for my bones are troubled.
My soul also is sorely troubled.
But thou, O Lord - how long?' (Vv.1-3)

The psalmist takes refuge in the loving mercy of God, in which he makes his act of faith. His personal insecurity is evident as he begins the journey. Just what is he to expect? In V.8-10 this act of faith is apparently rewarded and the psalmist once again finds himself restored to a new intimacy with God.

'Depart from me, all you workers of evil;
For the Lord has heard the sound of my weeping.
The Lord has heard my supplication;
The Lord accepts my prayer.
All my enemies shall be ashamed and sorely troubled;
They shall turn back, and be put to shame in a moment.'

In these two psalms we see the way the psalmist prayed. There was firstly the lament, the cry of one in pain. Then there was a moment when the psalmist made an act of faith that his prayer was heard and he entered into a new intimacy with God who heard the prayer of the psalmist. Then there was a moment of praise that constituted the response of the psalm to the presence of God.

In the psalms the psalmist expressed himself honestly about the way he felt and reached out as he found himself, not as he imagined himself to be; and this broken one is the one who reached out to God. Toni Craven [12] provides an interesting meditation on the emotional honesty of the psalmist. In many ways many of us are emotionally illiterate. Many have difficulty in naming feelings, 'owning' them and accepting and then coming to a healthy way of expressing them. The psalms provide a space, a place, where in the words of the psalmist we can name our feelings before God, understand them and in the new relationship struck with God come to a positive expression of ourselves. This is true of the psalms of lament.

One feeling that many of us are uncomfortable with is anger. Yet we see the psalmists angry at life and God and they express this in the psalms. In Psalm 44 we hear the community lament and protest:

> 'We have heard with our ears, O God,
> Our ancestors have told us,
> What deeds you performed in their days,
> In the days of old...
> Yet you have cast us off and abased us,
> And have not gone out with our armies.
> You have made us turn back from the foe;
> And our enemies have gotten spoil.
> You have made us like sheep for the slaughter,
> And scattered us among the nations ...
>
> All this had come upon us,
> Though we have not forgotten you,
> Or been false to your covenant ...
> Rouse yourself! Why do you sleep, O Lord?
> Awake! Do not cast us off for ever!' (Ps 44:1, 9-11, 17, 23)

We see here the emotional honesty of the people who feel abandoned and their anger at the situation in which they find themselves. In coming to terms with our anger and coming to an understanding of ourselves and what our emotions are telling us, the words of Harriet Goldhor Lerner provide us with food for thought:

'Thus, we too learn to fear our anger; not only because it brings about the disapproval of others, but also because it signals the necessity for change. We may begin to ask ourselves questions that serve to block or invalidate our own experience of anger: "Is my anger legitimate?" "Do I have a right to be angry?" "What's the use of my getting angry?" "What good will it do?" These questions can be excellent ways of silencing ourselves and shutting off our anger.

'Let us question these questions. Anger is neither legitimate nor illegitimate, meaningful nor pointless. Anger simply is. To ask, "Is my anger legitimate?" is similar to asking, "Do I have a right to be thirsty?" After all, I just had a glass of water fifteen minutes ago. Surely my thirst is not legitimate. And besides, what's the point of getting thirsty when I can't get anything to drink now, anyway?"

'Anger is something we feel. It exists for a reason and always deserves our respect and attention. We all have a right to *everything* we feel - and certainly our anger is no exception.' [13]

Expressions of anger and the way we feel allow the psalmists to become agents of change in relation to God, self and others. No matter what the cause, anger or other feelings are not suppressed in the psalms. All is surrendered into the hands of God who is present to those who pray. From the psalmists we learn that God stands ready to hear the one who prays and hears all that one has to say, whether we regard what we have to say as being OK in our books or not.

Walter Harelson gives an important distinction which helps one to live with what are often regarded as negative emotions. He distinguishes between angry thoughts and angry deeds:

'It is difficult to overestimate the importance of these laments. Viewed simply from the standpoint of the community's mental health, we can see how important it was that the community could address its laments and prayers to Yahweh without holding back its true feelings. Yahweh was ready, in their view, to hear their protestations. They could turn to Yahweh and state the simple facts of the experience. Yahweh might or might not come immediately to their aid, but at any rate nothing prevented them from saying exactly what they thought of Yahweh's governance of the universe ... Hatred of enemies is a basic element in human life. These psalmists did not, as we generally do, hide their hatred from the deity in their prayers.

'Is it not of much greater import to pray to God for vengeance against our enemies than to take vengeance into our own hands? [14]

Harelson points us in the direction of surrendering our feelings, which may also include hate, into the hands of God. He accepts us and comes to meet us in our brokenness no matter how this brokenness gives expression.

Michael Jinkens [15] performs the exercise of placing alongside the literary structure of the psalms of lament the stages of grief from Elizabeth Kubler-Ross. [16] He adds to this the stages outlined by Walter Brueggemann in the typology of the psalms. [17]

He draws the parallels between them in the following table:

Brueggemann's Typology of Psalms	Formal Structure of the Psalms	Kubler-Ross's Stages of Grief
Orientation	The prior state of health or wholeness or communal integration the loss of which forms the tacit backdrop for these psalms	Life prior to loss
Disorientation	Invocation (lamenting address to God) Cry of complaint Remembering God's Faithfulness Plea/Petition Confession of Trust	Denial and Isolation Anger/ Depression Bargaining
New Orientation	Words of Assurance/ Vows of Praise	Acceptance

The psalms of lament present us with an authentic portrayal of human suffering and the human emotions that arise when we are in distress. They help us to come to terms with our feelings and the situation in which we find ourselves. They provide a space where we can be ourselves and give expression to our human sorrows and suffering. As we learn from research into death and grief (Kubler-Ross), neglecting to honour the process of coming to terms with loss, making short-cuts to the establishment of equilibrium, seeking love in wrong places, for instance, on this painful journey only sustains denial and short-circuits our path to health and wholeness. We do not come to rest in God's peace. We do not find *shalom*. As Qoheleth reminds us: 'For everything there is a season, and a time for every matter under heaven.' (Ecc 3:1). There is time for feeling a sadness that disorientates us, for terror in the face of isolation and loneliness, for anger that rages and will not be ignored, for bargaining with God, and for depression that envelopes us in darkness. There is time for all these things and space to express them in the psalms.

This forms the background to understanding how we can emotionally lament before God, how we can surrender ourselves to God, trusting all the time in faith that we are heard and accepted. This is the way Jesus learned to pray and we see this in the Gethsemane scene we are looking at. Jesus is in the lives of his people He describes himself as being deeply grieved even unto death (Mk 14:38).

This is his act of faith and in praying thus he becomes prepared to meet his 'hour'. There is still an even more dramatic picture of Jesus praying the lament and we now come to the special place of Ps22 in the passion of Jesus.

Jesus and Ps 22

The theme of Jesus' praying as the ones of old prayed the psalms of lament is dramatically presented by Mark when he speaks of the death of Jesus. Mark tells us:

'When the sixth hour came there was darkness over the whole land until the ninth hour. And at the last hour Jesus cried out in a loud voice, "*Eloi, Eloi, lama sabachthani?*" which means "My God, my God, why have you forsaken me?" ' (15:33ff)

The words '*Eloi, Eloi, lama sabachthani*' are Aramaic, the dialect of Hebrew that Jesus spoke. Carroll Stuhmueller narrates an event in his life that might help throw light on Jesus' use of this psalm. [18] He tells of the death of his mother. When he arrived at the hospital he was told that she was speaking gibberish but when he reached her he recognised that she was praying in her native tongue. The prayers she had learned when she was young came back to her and in her last agony these were the ones she prayed. Stuhmueller sees in this a model for helping us understand Jesus.

Mark quotes the Aramaic words used by Jesus because of the impression these words made on his followers. Stuhmueller suggests that Jesus, in his last agony, prayed the way he had been taught as a child and the prayer that came to him was the prayer of lament, Ps 22. Jesus reverted to a prayer that must have been of comfort to him and he found Ps 22 to be appropriate.

When Michael Jinkins speaks about Psalm 22 he entitles it 'The God-forsakedness of God'. [19] Psalm 22 is a classic psalm of lament. Here I quote it in full (NRSV).

'My God, my God, why have you forsaken me?

Why are you so far from
helping me; from the
words of my groaning?
O my God, I cry by day; but
you do not answer;
and by night, but find no rest.

84

Yet you are holy,
enthroned on the praises of Israel.
In you our ancestors trusted;
they trusted, and you
delivered them.
To you thy cried, and were saved;
In you they trusted, and were
not put to shame.

But I am a worm, and not human;
scorned by others, and
despised by the people.
All who see me mock at me;
They make mouths at me, they
shake their heads:
"Commit your cause to the
Lord; let him deliver -
let him rescue the one in
whom he delights!"

Yet it was you who took me
from the womb;
you kept me safe on my
mother's breast.
On you I was cast from my birth,
And since my mother bore me
you have been my God.
Do not be far from me.
for trouble is near
and there is no one to help.

Many bulls encircle me,
strong bulls of Bashan
surround me;
they open wide their mouths at me,
like a ravening and roaring lion.

I am poured out like water,
and all my bones are out of joint;
My heart is like wax;
it is melted within my breast;
my mouth is dried up like a potsherd,
And my tongue sticks to my jaws;
You lay me in the dust of death.

For dogs are all around me;
a company of evildoers
encircles me.
My hands and feet have shrivelled;
I can count all my bones.
they stare and gloat over me;
they divide my clothes among themselves,
and for my clothing they cast lots.

But you, O Lord, do not be far away!
O my help, come quickly to my aid!
Deliver my soul from the sword,
my life, from the power of the dog!
Save me from the mouth of the lion!
from the horns of the old oxen
you have rescued me.
I will tell of your name to my
brothers and sisters;
in the midst of the
congregation I will praise you
you who fear the Lord, praise him!
all you offspring of Jacob
glorify him;
Stand in awe of him, all you
offspring of Israel!
for he did not despise or abhor
the affliction of the afflicted;
he did not hide his face from me,
but heard when I cried to him.

From you comes my praise in
the great congregation;
my vows I will pay before
those who fear him;
the poor shall eat and be satisfied;
those who seek him shall
praise the Lord.
May your hearts live forever!

All the ends of the earth shall
remember
and turn to the Lord;
and all the families of the nations
shall worship before him.
For dominion belongs to the Lord,
and he rules over the nations.

To him, indeed shall all who
sleep in the earth bow down;
before him shall bow all who
go down to the dust,
and I shall live for him.
Posterity will serve him;
future generations will be told
about the Lord;
and proclaim his deliverance to
a people yet unborn,
saying that he has done it.

Psalm 22 initially comes from an individual sufferer but it
becomes the property of the 'great congregation' of the
'afflicted' in Israel, each influencing the other and by sharing
their spirit contributing to the inspiration of the Bible. [20] From
the ranks of the innocent, hopeful community comes Jesus
who turned to this psalm in his agony. At the root of the psalm
is a basic 'I - thou' relationship between the psalmist and God.
We see this in the following way in which the psalmist begins

lines: 'My God ... Why art Thou ... O my God ... Yet, then ... In thee ... Yet then ... But thou, O Lord."

Vv. 1-12 form the individual lament. V.1 sees the psalmist address God, asking Him why he has forsaken the psalmist. We never feel abandoned by those we regard as strangers but when those we love appear to have abandoned us we feel this pain intensely. In v.2 the psalmist cries out that God does not listen to him. He no longer hears the ones he loves. Later on in the psalm we hear the psalmist tell us that he is a worm and not human, he is scorned by others, and defied by the people (v.6). He describes his situation as being surrounded by 'strong bulls' (v.12) and he describes himself as being 'poured out like water' (v.14), his mouth as 'dried up like a potsherd' (v.15). Through these images which the psalmist communicates, he laments his situation before God. In v.3-5 the psalmist recalls that God was faithful in the past but past remembrance makes the situation of the psalmist appear lonelier still.

The long lament ends with the prayer found in Vv.19-21, where the final word in the Hebrew is 'You have heard me'. There we see Cox's idea of meeting God in the situation one finds oneself in, and the concept of the psalm as sacramental (see above). The psalmist is calm again because he has been heard. This is perhaps where some people (and I include myself) encounter difficulties. I can relate to the first fact of the lament where my pain causes me to cry out to God and lament that he has forsaken me. It is not easy to believe that in praying the psalm, I enter the presence of God who hears me and meets me where I am. It is the model of Jesus praying the psalm that helps us pray these verses. He called out to God, asking him why he had forsaken him; but all the time he held on to his faith in the God of Israel and surrendered himself into His hands. We see this fidelity in the Gethsemane scene (Mk14: 32-42) and then the prayer of lament, Ps 22, appears in the last words on the cross (Mk 15:33). Always implicit in the psalm of lament is entrusting oneself to God who, however obscurely, hears the one who prays thus. Jesus lived out the faith in his relationship with the one he called 'Abba'. He had to reach out beyond his pain and anger and believe that in the end he was heard.

In Mk 16 we come to the empty tomb and learn that Jesus has been raised (16:6) and he has gone before his disciples to Galilee (16:7), effecting a reconciliation with the disciples and Peter. In this we see that Jesus' prayer was answered; he was vindicated by God.

In the song of thanksgiving (Vv. 22-26) we see in the ritual invoked that both the original psalmist and Yahweh live together in the assembly at prayer. The psalm enables the past and the present to merge in one act of worship and so proclaim now that presence of Yahweh, who continues to live in the words of scripture and the action of the liturgy. [21]

The second song of thanksgiving (Vv. 27-31) manifests the continued life of the psalmist where lament becomes a prayer of thanksgiving for the 'great congregation' of the 'afflicted'. Others who are afflicted are now summoned to participate in the prayer of Ps 22. The psalmist is in solidarity with those who are afflicted. He shows compassion to them. He is broken and calls others who are broken to come to new life and meaning just as he has himself. Jesus himself prayed this way and his prayers were heard. (cf. Heb 5:7) He is compassionate to those who suffer, he shares their pain and we are told he 'became the source of eternal salvation for all that obey him'. (Heb 5:9).

The words of Psalm 22 serve as the final words of Jesus in the Gospel. In Mark's gospel as a whole, there can be no question that these words are an expression of faith, not despair or bitterness. [22] The opening line of the psalm is to be understood in the context of the whole psalm. The words on the cross are the completed form of Jesus' prayer in Gethsemane, which also took the form of a lament. Jesus affirmed there his unbroken love for the Father while experiencing the full terror of approaching death (cf. 14:32-42).

However, the very fact that Mark makes Jesus' words a lament must not be downplayed. The words emphasise the feeling of torment and abandonment that Jesus felt. In Mark's account Jesus dies in agony with a wordless scream on his lips (Mk 15:37). Jesus' trust in God is not broken but Mark shows us the fierce assault of death and abandonment.

The early Christian communities, through whom the gospel narratives came into being, identified Jesus as the one who laments in the psalms. Raymond Brown [23] describes Ps 22 as the Crucifixion Psalm. He produces the following parallels between Ps 22 and the passion narratives. [24] (In the interest of completeness I include reference to other Passion narratives apart from Mark's):

1* Ps 22:2a: 'My God, my God, receive me, to what purpose have you forsaken me?' In having Jesus quote this, Matt 27:46 is slightly closer to the septugint wording than is Mark 15:34, but neither quotes the italicised phrase, which is also absent from the Masoretic Text.

2* Ps 22:3, 'My God, I have shouted ... by night, and there is not rest for me' may be alluded to in the Synoptic pattern of darkness over the whole earth to the ninth hour when Jesus uttered a loud cry (Mark 15:33-34; Matt 27:45-46; Luke 23:44, 46).

3* Ps 22:7b, 'Reviled [*oneidizein*] by human beings and considered as nothing [*exouthenein*] by people' is plausibly alluded to in the mockery of Jesus on the cross where Mark 15:29, 32b and Matt 17:39,44 have the passers-by blaspheme him and the co-crucified 'revile' him. In Luke 23:11 Herod treats Jesus as nothing (ie 'with contempt').

4* Ps22:8a, 'All those observing me sneered at me' is probably alluded to in the Lucan form (23:35a) of the mockery of Jesus on the cross: 'And the people were standing there observing. But there were also rulers sneering.'

5* Ps 22:8b, 'They spoke with the lips; they wagged the head' is probably alluded to in Mark 15:29; Matt 27-39 where those passing by are 'wagging their heads'.

6* Ps 22:9, 'He hoped in the Lord; let Him deliver him; let Him save him because He wants him' is partially echoed in the challenge to Jesus on the cross: 'Save yourself' (Mark 15:30; Matt 27:40; Luke 23:39b). It is more fully echoed in Matt 27:43: 'He has trusted God. Let him be delivered if He wants him.'

7* Ps 22:16b, 'My tongue has stuck to my jaws' may be part of the background of John 19:28 where, in order that the Scripture be completed, Jesus says, 'I thirst.' (See also Pss 42:2-3; 69:4).

8* Ps 22:17b, 'A company of evildoers [*poneroumenoi*] has encircled me' may lie behind depicting the crucified Jesus between two bandits (Mark 15:27; Matt 27:38; cf. John 19:18), especially in Luke 23:33: 'They crucified him and the wrongdoers [*kakourgoi*], the one on the right and the other on the left.'

9* Ps 22:17c, 'They have pierced my hands and my feet' is probably echoed in the portrait of the crucified, risen Jesus in Luke 24:39, 'See my hands and my feet (cf. John 20L25,27: 'the place of the nails ... see my hands').

10* Ps 22:19, 'They divided up my clothes among themselves, and for my clothing they threw lots' lies behind the description of the division of the crucified Jesus' clothes in all four Gospels, and appears verbatim as a fulfilment citation in John 19:24.

11* Ps 22:25c, 'And in my shouting [*kragein*] to Him, He heard me' may be alluded to in the Synoptic sequence where, when Jesus has expired with a loud cry (*phone*), divine intervention takes place with the rending of the sanctuary veil (Mark 15:37-38; Matt 27:54; Luke 23:46,45b).

12* Ps 22:28b, 'All the families of the nations shall worship before Him' may be remotely alluded to in the reaction of the

(Gentile) centurion confessing Jesus who had just died (Mark 15:39; Matt 27:54; Luke 23:47).

In praying Ps 22, Jesus made it his own; it is his prayer. Christ took the prayer to himself and in him it acquired its full meaning. [25] In summing up we can say that the first Christian community lived in the atmosphere of the psalms and Ps 22 became the psalm of the Passion. The spirituality of Ps 22 permeates the whole of the Passion Narratives. Claus Westermann [26] sums up all this in the following words:

'In this psalm the depth of the lamentor's vexation and temptation to despair and the miracle of the reversal of his suffering come to unique expression. By taking into himself this last trial of being forsaken by God, Christ descended into the depth of human isolation and made our suffering his suffering to its depths. The despairing questions of those who suffer in our world (Why? How long?) are questions that were known by him in whom God's goodness became human. They are not foreign to him. He took our suffering as part of his suffering to the fullest possible extent. Psalm 22 ... was taken up into the passion story as a representative of psalms of lament in general ... If, however, Psalm 22 was incorporated into the passion story, then such incorporation must include the entire psalm. For viewed in its totality, Psalm 22 is a lament which has been reversed. Its second part (from V.22 on) is praise by a person who has been delivered, praise that has anticipated the actual deliverance. Just as it can be said in the second part of Psalm 22,

"For he has not despised or abhorred the affliction of
    the afflicted;
and he has not hid his face from him, but has heard,
    when he cried to him ... (V.24)",

so, similarly, the proclamation of the earliest messengers of the resurrection was full of the message that God responded to the cry from the cross. The message of Easter is narrative praise. It is possible that the phrase that appears in Matthew's Easter account, 'go and tell my brethren' (Matt 28:10), is an allusion to the beginning of the second part of Psalm 22, 'I will tell of thy name to my brethren."

Lament and our Situation Today

The prayer of lament is appropriate for many of us today. So often we can feel a welter of emotions and feel as if we are out of control. Many of us are afraid to admit that we can be angry and unforgiving, keeping resentment in and all the while allowing it to fester until we come to the point when our pain will no longer be ignored. We can end up dumping our anger on the wrong person, the one we should love most of all. We can also develop symptoms of physical illness, which is really an interior pain calling out for healing, but which has been ignored for too long.

In our own day we are becoming more aware of the interior pain that so many people are in. The figures for suicide alone bear testimony to this. I do not intend here to give a scientific answer that would show where all interior pain comes from, I meditate only on one way in which people are hurt.

It has come to light recently how many people have suffered from sexual abuse. These people carry deep wounds in them. They feel guilty, dirty and worthless. These are 'wounds' that will not go away. It has also come to light that many of the abusers were in positions of trust and respect (I am thinking here of people in the service of the Church). The ones abused are also Church. Nobody resembles Christ more than the innocents who suffer. In some cases I have come across, when good people reported their suspicions of wrongdoing, they found they were not heard and they found no relief from their pain. Nothing was done. They learned the harsh lesson that indifference is even worse than hatred. These experiences have left people hurt, sad and angry. Many other people in our world are lonely for many other reasons. They feel that they do not matter. The causes for all the loneliness in our world are manifold. Suffice to say, loneliness is a real state in which many find themselves.

So we see that the reasons for lament are there. Praying in the spirit of Jesus and in the spirit of the psalms of old is one possible way to begin the journey to healing. The one who prays the 'lament' is the one who can name his/her experience. These words may name the experience of anger, sadness, shame, depression and loneliness. In naming the experience they come to 'own' their emotions and begin the journey to understanding their feelings. In the prayer of lament I express the way I feel, the way I find life. In doing this I come to express my deepest feelings and ones which I may not feel at home with. Many of us find it difficult to come to terms with any anger. In my prayer I tell God the way I find things and complain to him about His absence when the pain is at its most intense.

Then comes what is for me the most difficult part. It is a long journey to owning and understanding my feelings, but even more difficult is the step of affirming my faith that God hears my prayer and will lead me to a new relationship with him, where I will experience a resurrection in my life. There I do not rely on my own energy but I look to Jesus who prayed the 'lament' on his cross. He was able to reach out through his pain and with him as the one who compassionates with me, I take faltering steps in affirming that my prayer is heard. God, however obscurely, hears me and in love comes to me where I am and as I am. I come to experience the peace (*shalom*) of God who meets me in my pain. I journey with the lonely Christ from Gethsemane through Calvary to the resurrection.

NOTES ON CHAPTER 4

1. R Pesh, *Das Markusevangelium* (Freiburg/Basel/Wien: 3rd revised edition, 1980:2 Vols) Pesh appeals to this motif as a basic ingredient of Mark's passion narrative.

2. D Senior, *The Passion of Jesus in the Gospel of Mark* (Collegeville, MN: Michael Glazier 1984) p.72.

3. PD Miller, Jr., Trouble and Woe Interpreting Biblical Laments. Interpretation (1983), 32-45 contains a discussion on the theology of lament and its use in the passion narrative.

4. James Luther Mays, *The Lord Reigns: A Theological Handbook to the Psalms* (Louisville: Westminster: John Knox Press 1994) p.6.

5. Ibid. p.6.

6. Ibid., p.7.

7. Ibid., p.10

8. Ludwig Wittgenstein, *Philosophical Investigation* (translated by GEM Anscombe: New York: Macmillan, 1958 ed.) p.8.

9. D Cox, *The Psalms in the Life of God's People* (Slough: St Paul's Publications: 1984), p 2f.

10. D Cox, op. cit. p.4-9

11. ibid, p.68.

12. T Craven, *The Book of Psalms* (Collegeville MN: Michael Glazier 1992) pp47-55.

13. HG Lerner, *The Dance of Anger* (New York: Harper and Row: 1985) p 3-4.

14. W Harleson, *Interpreting the Old Testament* (New York: Holt Rinehart and Winston, Inc. 1964) p.415.

15. M Jinkins, *In the House of the Lord* (Collegeville, MN: Liturgical Press: 1998), p.118.

16. The stages of grief can be found in E. Kubler-Ross, *On Death and Dying* (New York: Macmillan: 1969).

17. W. Brueggmann, *The Message of the Psalms* (Minneapolis: Augsburg: 1984).

18. Carroll Stuhmeuller, *Retreat with the Psalms* (audio cassettes) (Cafield, Ohio: Alba House Cassettes; 1993) tape 5.

19. M. Jinkins, N(15), p.101.

20. C Stuhmueller, Psalms 1, (Wilmington Delawere: Glazier, 1983) p.147.

21. C Stuhmueller, op. cit., p.150

22. See the comments of F Matera, *The Kinship of Jesus: Composition of Theology of Mk 15* (Chico CA: Scholars Press 1982) p.132-135.

23. R E Brown, *The Death of the Messiah, Vol.2* (London: Chapman 1993) p.1462.

24. Ibid. p.1460-1462.

25. D Bonhoeffer, *Prayerbook of the Bible* (Minneapolis: Fortress Press, 1996) p.166.

26. C.Westermann, *The Psalms: Structure, Content and Message* (Minneapolis: Augsberg: 1980), p.125-126.

CHAPTER 5

JESUS AND PRAYER

The Prayer of Jesus in Gethsemane

In Gethsemane we see Jesus face to face with death. He is horrified and shocked. We hear the words of Jesus' prayer. We are told:

'And going on a little farther, he fell on the ground and prayed that if it were possible, the hour might pass from him. And he said 'Abba, Father, all things are possible for thee; remove this cup from me; yet not what I will , but what thou wilt.' (14:35-36)

In the garden at the Mount of Olives, Mark's use of the wilderness theme comes to a climax. Jesus, the New Samuel, began his ministry by repeating the exodus pattern, passing through the waters and out into the wilderness, the place of testing and grace. Repeatedly throughout his ministry Jesus re-established his identification with the wilderness either in the wilderness itself or in other wilderness places, such as the mountain or the sea. The Gethsemane passage is one of the three passages in Mark that show Jesus praying and all take place at night and in the wilderness (here on the mountain). Augustine Stock makes the following comment: 'In Mark the wilderness passages follow descriptions of the teaching and healing ministry of Jesus or his disciples. The activity represents the accomplishment of Jesus' mission - the confrontation will not be an unbroken series of successes, triumphs. Quite the contrary. As Jesus' self-disclosure unfolds, it becomes increasingly clear that Jesus must fulfil his mission by way of vicarious sacrifice, and that for him the way to victory runs through humiliation, suffering, death and apparent total defeat.'[1]

The other passages where Jesus went into the wilderness to pray prepare us for the Gethsemane scene and the prayer Jesus offers. We are also prepared to see the reaction of the disciples. In Chapter 1 we read:

'And in the morning, a great while before day, he rose and went out to a lonely place, and there he prayed. And Simon and those who were with him followed him. And they found him and said to him, "Every one is searching for you". And he said to them, "Let us go on to the next towns, that I may preach there also; for that is why I came out." And he went throughout all Galilee, preaching in their synagogues and casting out demons.' (1:35-39)

Jesus went off to a lonely place (*eis erémon topon*). We are inclined to think of this as a desert place but the country around Capernaum was cultivated in Jesus' time. This serves to remind us that in Mark's wilderness theology; 'wilderness' means 'isolated places'. Jesus has been carrying out his public mission, preaching and healing. Then he withdraws to a wilderness spot. It is here that he prays. [2] It is in such wilderness areas that Jesus comes to know who he is and his relationship with God. Here in Prayer Jesus is with his Father. Even though at this stage we do not know the context of Jesus' prayer, we do know that after his encounter with the one he loved, he entered the world of others filled with compassion. This compassion is revealed in his preaching and healing of broken bodies and minds. Charles De Foucauld says the following in a letter written to a trappist: 'To receive the grace of God, you must go to a desert place and stay awhile. There you can be emptied of and unburdened of everything that does not pertain to God. There the house of your soul is swept clean to make room for God. We need this silence, this absence of every creature, so that God can build his hermitage within us.'[3]

Also in this passage we are presented with the figure of Peter. We are told: 'Simon ... followed him [*katedioxen*].' Mary Ann Tolbert [4] suggests that *katedioxen* be translated as 'hunted him down' rather than 'followed him' or 'searched him out'.

The word carries a strong, hostile connotation. Simon and the others harassed Jesus and tracked him down. John Dominic Crossan[5] suggests an unworthy motive for Peter's acting this way. He says any Mediterranean person would recognise what should happen or what is already happening. Peters' house became a brokerage place for Jesus' healings, and Peter would broker between Jesus and those seeking help. Whether this is true or not I don't know but what is clear from the passage is that Peter was concerned with other things and does not understand the need Jesus had to be alone and pray. There is more than a hint of anger in his seeking out of Jesus.

Later on we see Jesus at prayer, once again alone, but we also sense the growing gap between Jesus and the disciples.

'And at once he made his disciples get into the boat and go on ahead to the other side near Bethsaida, while he himself sent the crowd away. After saying goodbye to them he went off into the mountain to pray. When evening came, the boat was far out in the middle of the sea, and he was alone on the land. He could see they were distressed in rowing, for the wind was against them; and about the fourth watch of the night he came towards them, walking on the sea. He was going to pass them by but when they saw him walking on the sea they thought it was a ghost and cried out; for they had all seen him and were terrified. But at once he spoke to them and said, "Courage! It's me! Do not be afraid." Then he got into the boat with them and the wind dropped. They were utterly and completely dumbfounded, because they had not seen what the miracle of the loaves meant; their hearts were hardened.' (6:45-52)

Here we see Jesus go away to pray. This incident comes after the feeding of the five thousand. Once again Mark leaves a gap in his narrative. We are not told the content of Jesus' prayer. This is left to the readers to fill in for themselves. What we know from Mark is that such time is precious to Jesus but the disciples do not understand this.

The disciples go without Jesus. Whenever he is absent from them (or appears to be so, as when he was asleep during a storm in 4:35) they find themselves in distress. Night is a time for Jesus' prayer to his Father but for the disciples darkness signifies their confused state of mind. They do not understand Jesus' feeding of the multitude. Their hearts are petrified. As Mark says, 'their hearts were hardened' (6:52). They were not open to any new insights or new ways of understanding Jesus and the world.

Robert Fowler [6] notes the following; He points to the fact that Mark uses doublets to emphasise his point. There are two instances of storms at sea. In 4:35-41, Jesus stills the storm at sea. Here he comes to the disciples at sea. Rather than feeling empathy for the grief-stricken disciples, we cannot help judging them unfavourably. They do not recognise who is coming to them. Nor do they seem to remember the incident in 4:35-41 where they woke Jesus from sleep and where he calmed the storm at sea. They do not recognise who the one must be, 'that even wind and sea obey him'. (4:41). There is a heightened sense of alienation between Jesus and his disciples here.

In Chapter 9 we have another story of healing, but the healing also teaches us indirectly about prayer. We learn about the disciples' attitude as against the attitude of Jesus:

'And he asked them, "What are you arguing about with them?" A man answered him from the crowd, "Master, I have brought my son to you; there is a spirit of dumbness in him, and when it takes hold of him it throws him to the ground, and he foams at the mouth and grinds his teeth and goes rigid. And I asked your disciples to drive it out and they were unable to."

'In reply he said to them, "You faithless generation, how much longer must I be among you? How much longer must I put up with you? Bring him to me." They brought the boy to him, and at once the spirit of dumbness threw the boy into convulsions, and he fell to the ground and lay writhing there, foaming at the mouth. Jesus asked the father, "How long has this been happening to him?"

' "From childhood," he said, "and it has often thrown him into fire and into water, in order to destroy him. But if you can do anything, have pity on us and help us."

' "If you can?" retorted Jesus. "Everything is possible for one who has faith." At once the father of the boy cried out, "I have faith. Help my lack of faith!" And when Jesus saw that a crowd was gathering, he rebuked the unclean spirit. "Deaf and dumb spirit," he said, "I command you: come out of him and never enter him again!" Then it threw the boy into violent convulsions and came out shouting, and the boy lay there so like a corpse that most of them said, "He is dead." But Jesus took him by the hand and helped him up, and he was able to stand.

'When he had gone indoors, his disciples asked him when they were by themselves, "Why were we unable to drive it out?" He replied, "This is the kind that can only be driven out by prayer." ' (9:16-29)

The spirit that attacks the boy is initially described as a spirit of dumbness, rendering him incapable of sharing in human speech. This contrasts with the verbal argumentation that had been going on among the disciples and now among the crowd. The exasperated father tells Jesus that the disciples were unable to heal the boy. He asks Jesus if he can, take pity on the boy. Another translation is even more correct; instead of 'take pity on us' we could have the expression 'have compassion on us'. Jesus retorts that everything is possible for the one who has faith and he heals the boy. When the disciples question him as to why they could not heal the boy Jesus replies, 'This is the kind that can only be driven out by prayer' (9:29), the implication is obvious: the disciples did not pray. However there is no mention of Jesus praying either. What are we to assume? From the earlier passages quoted (1:35, 6:46) we saw that Jesus had a habit of prayer. From his prayer flowed his healing power.

There is something else implicit in the conversation between Jesus and the distracted father. He had asked Jesus to have compassion on them (9:23). Jesus had compassion on them

101

and healed the boy. There is an implicit link set up between prayer and compassion. From Jesus' time alone with his father comes his compassion for his suffering brothers and sisters. His compassion is an expression of his relationship with God. There is an explicit link in the passage between faith and the healing. The distracted father is told that everything is possible for the one who has faith. The father gathers up his courage in the face of disappointment and tells Jesus, 'I have faith. Help my lack of faith.' (9:24).

By faith, we allow God to enter our situation of pain.

* * * * *

In Chapter 11, after the scene of the fig tree and the so-called cleansing of the temple, we find Jesus use this as an opportunity to give a brief cathesis on prayer.

'Next morning as they passed by, they saw the fig tree withered to the roots. Peter remembered, "Look, Rabbi," he said to Jesus, "the fig tree that you cursed has withered away." Jesus answered, "Have faith in God. In truth I tell you, if anyone says to this mountain: Be pulled up and thrown into the sea, with no doubt in his heart, but believing that what he says will happen, it will be done for him. I tell you therefore, everything you ask and pray for, believe that you have it already, and it will be yours. And when you stand in prayer, forgive whatever you have against anyone, so that your Father in heaven may forgive your failings too." ' (11:20-25).

The cleansing of the temple represents Jesus' prophetic act of ending cultic worship for his disciples within the temple. This symbolic act points to a new form of divine worship which will have personal, ethical and social components. This is the new era inaugurated by Jesus, who tells his disciples, 'If anyone says to this mountain ...' Jesus tells him that if they pray with no doubt then they are to believe that they have already received what they ask for in faith. Only trust in divine guidance can overcome the bewilderment that has just overcome Peter and his companions. Mark has retained the thought (faith can work the seemingly impossible) and then in an interjected clause ('with no doubt ... but believes') has added an exhortation to firmness of faith. Prayer is meant to be seen as a way of life for Jesus' disciples. Faith becomes public and concrete in community prayer. This is then linked by Jesus to the act of forgiveness 'so that your father may forgive your failings too.' (11:25). We see Jesus pray in Gethsemane. For the first time in Mark we hear that content of Jesus' prayer and what he asks for in prayer is not heard.

Mark has indicated by inference that for Jesus the time he spent with God was crucial for him. Now we can share in the depth of this relationship by sharing in Jesus' lonely vigil.

'And going on a little further he threw himself on the ground and prayed that if it were possible the hour might pass him by. "Abba, Father!" he said "For you everything is possible. Take this cup away from me. But not what I will, but what you will " ' (14:35-36)

We get further indications of the anguish Jesus was in. Mark tells us of Jesus throwing himself on the ground in an excess of emotion. We hear two accounts of the content of Jesus' prayer. Both accounts reinforce one another. The first account is given in indirect discourse and the second is given in direct discourse.

In the indirect discourse Jesus prays that the hour might pass him by (14:35). A few verses later Jesus will interpret the hour as the time when the Son of Man will be handed over into the hands of sinners (V.41). The hour here had a meaning in historical time. The 'hour' is also used by Jesus in another sense. In Mark 13:32 it signals the time when the signs of the final age take place. The sense of ultimate encounter between good and evil is called the 'eschatological' time.

The idea that the hour of Gethsemane is eschatological is strengthened when we note that throughout the gospel Jesus encounters the opposition of Satan, unclean spirits and demonic forces when he preaches the kingdom (1:13, 23, 32, 39-, 4:15; 5:8; 6:7, 13; 7:25 etc) Particularly important is 3:22-

27 where Jesus envisages a kingdom of Satan and the conquest of that kingdom by the stronger one. Also important is 8:33 where Peter's suggestion that the Son of Man must not face suffering is rejected as Satanic. In this sense the scene of Gethsemane is seen as the ultimate encounter between good and evil. This is the sense in which the scene is called eschatological.

Jesus' prayer does not alter the course of events. The 'hour' does not pass him by. The 'hour' is not directly organised by God. The state of Jesus shows him involved in a real situation. His goodness and preaching have brought about rejection and violence. Jesus is immersed in the complexities of life at their worst. Earlier in the gospel Jesus is detached in his announcements of the passion, but now he is in turmoil as he prays the hour might pass him by.

In the vocalised prayer of Jesus we hear him say: 'Abba Father. All things are possible for you. Take away this cup from me. But not what I will, but what you will.' (14:36). In the outlook of biblical figures it was not irreverent to ask God for a change of mind. Moses interceded to ask the Lord to change his mind over Israel after the incident of the golden calf (Ex 32:10-14). Hezekiah prays to God to change his mind about his death (2 Kings 20:1-6), and the story of David crossing the Kidron valley (2 Sam 15:25-26) is also worth noting. Having crossed the Kidron River, David sends Zadok with the ark back to Jerusalem. Then David hopes that he too will be brought back but if this is not to be so, he prays 'let him deal with me as he likes'. In 1 Macc 3:58-60 Judas encourages his troops to battle if it be according to God's will in Heaven. Such instances of prayer show a trust in God and are not signs of rebellion. Jesus is in the spirit of these Old Testament figures.

J Gilbert [7] finds a four-fold division in the prayer of Jesus: (a) invocation (b) confession (c) request and (d) dedication to the will of God.

(a) Invocation: Jesus addresses his prayer to God when he calls *Abba*, which is translated as Father for the Greek-speaking audience of Mark's Gospel. Gal 4:6 and Rom 8:15

bear witness to the fact that the early Christian communities addressed God as *Abba*. The word *Abba* itself is a transliteration of an original Aramaic word. Aramaic was the language spoken by Jesus and the fact that the word is preserved in its Aramaic form illustrates the depth of the effect Jesus' words had on the disciples. In Mark's text it is accompanied by the Greek equivalent '*ho pater.*'

Much of the discussion about the meaning of *Abba* has developed in debate with the work of Joaichim Jeremias. [8] His position is that when Jesus addresses God as *Abba* he is showing that there exists an intimate family relationship between God and himself. Jeremias argues that no one has produced a single instance from Palestinian Judaism in which God is addressed as 'Father' by an individual. [9]

However, there is evidence from the Dead Sea Scrolls of Quamran of an author addressing God in Hebrew as 'My Father' (4Q372) and in the Greek Old-Testament (LXX) there are instances of people praying to the one they called Father but we cannot assume that these expressions translate as *Abba*. The word *Abba* used by Jesus is normal for a more intimate relationship such as that between a child and its father. It is plausible to say that Jesus' address to God in Aramaic was both a historical and memorable (because unusual) practice of Jesus himself reflecting the close relationship that existed between God and himself.

John Ashton states his conclusion as follows: 'The personal sense of the fatherhood of God was a typically Christian development of the Judaic tradition, and this probably originated in a recollection of Jesus' teaching and the example of his own prayer.'[10] JA Fitzmyer has analysed the expression *Abba* and he too states that there is no evidence for anyone using *Abba* as a form of personal address to God.[11]

The term *Abba* is not meant to indicate sex but rather to emphasize the uniqueness of Jesus' close relationship to God. God is neither male nor female and is beyond creatorly images. God embodies and is greater than the best characteristics of men and women - the fullness of fatherhood and motherhood.

Metaphors for God could be male or female. Our language about God indicates our efforts to come to terms with the mystery of God and express in a human way our relationship with Him, who is always greater than our categories.

In a passage from the thanksgiving hymns from Quamran the fatherly and motherly images for God come together beautifully: 'For thou art a father to all of Thy truth, and as a woman who tenderly loves her babe, so dost O Thou rejoice in them: and as a foster-father bearing a child in his lap, so carest Thou for all thy creatures.' (1Q H9:34-35) [12]

Evelyn Underhill [13] looked at the idea of fatherhood of God long before the current discussion. She says that the idea of fatherhood so central to Christian mysticism can be easily degraded into anthropomorphism of the sentimental kind. To escape this anthropomorphism she goes to the nameless mystic who writes in the *Theologia Germanica* (cap.53):

'Christ hath also said: "No man cometh unto Me, except the Father, which hath sent Me, draw him." Now mark: by the Father, I understand the Perfect, Simple Good, which is All and above All, and without which and besides which there is no true Substance, nor true Good, and without which no good work ever was or will be done. And in that it is All, it must be in All and above All ... Now behold, when this Perfect Good, which is unnameable, floweth into a Person able to bring forth, and bringeth forth the Only-begotten Son in that Person, and itself in Him, we call it the Father.'

(b) Confession: Jesus goes on to say, 'All things are possible for you.' He recognises how powerful is the one he addresses as *Abba*. He has the faith and trust of a true son. When Jesus told the disciples how hard it would be for a rich man to enter the kingdom (10:46) he immediately went on to say that all things are possible for God. In 11:24 he told his disciples that whatever they asked for in prayer they would receive. The indirect statement of V.35 ('if it is possible ...') contains the germ of the idea that what is happening is somehow in accord with God's purpose and Jesus might have to submit to his tragic fate. [14]

(c) Request: Jesus asks God to take away this 'cup' from him. This parallels the request in indirect speech that the hour pass him by. The two requests have the literary effect of reinforcing each other. However, there are special nuances and shades of meaning to the word 'cup'. There are five Old Testament meanings for it and with one exception ('a cup [sap] of reeling' in Zech 12:2), only *kôs* is used metaphorically. [15] The Greek word *poterion* translates *kôs* thirty out of thirty-three times in the Greek Old-Testament (LXX). The idea of the word 'cup' being used to describe the cup of God's wrath to be drunk by all the guilty is found in the ancient near-east. [16] Usually it refers to concrete historical punishments (eg Is 51:7; Jer 25:15-16; 51:7; Ez 23:33, Ps.79) In the New Testament Rev 14:10 and 16:19 show that an apocalyptic cup of wrath can be envisaged. This use of the word 'cup' leads to the question: is God trying to make Jesus the object of His anger? Is he to drink the cup of God's anger? It is therefore necessary to look at the other possible meanings of cup.

RE Brown [17] says that others have understood the 'cup' which Jesus prayed would be his fate or destiny. There is some Old Testament evidence for the Hebrew word *kôs* as the positive good portion allotted to the writer (e.g. Ps 116:5; 23:5; 116:13). The word 'cup' can by analogy refer to a negative fate. We find each usage in the Targums. These are Aramaic translations or paraphrases of the Hebrew Old Testament. Tasting of the cup of death is found in the targum Neofiti of Deut 32:1, and in Neofiti, Yerushalmi II and the fragmentary targum of Gen 40:23. [18] In some of the manuscripts of the 'Testament of Abraham' 16:2 we find the expression 'the bitter cup of death'. In the 'Martyrdom of Polycarp 14:2' the cup is a sharing in the martyrdom of Christ leading to resurrection. The Martyrdom of Isaiah (late 1st century AD) refers to the prophet as saying 'Only for me has God mixed this cup.' Thus in comparative Jewish literature we find the cup referring to a negative fate.

Even more pertinent to the discussion of the meaning of the word cup is Jesus' question to James and John in Mk

10:38-39: 'Are you able to drink the cup that I drink or be baptised with the baptism with which I am baptised?' The two disciples had just asked to be given places of honour, one at the right and the other at the left, in Jesus' kingdom. The simplest explanation of 10:38-39 is that the disciples are being offered the cup of suffering that Jesus is to drink. Ironically, at Jesus' cross it is two thieves who are placed, one on the right and the other on the left (15:37). The disciples are being asked if they can accept the affliction that the proclamation of the kingdom involves. The words of Jesus in 8:34 are relevant here: 'If anyone comes after me, let him take up his cross and follow me.' We can say therefore that the cup Jesus refers to in 14:36 is the suffering of a horrendous death as part of a great trial. Some of the connotations of the classical cup of wrath are still present, not in the sense that Jesus is the object of God's anger but in the sense that his death takes place in the apocalyptic struggle of the end -time when God's kingdom overcomes evil. It therefore has both a historical and an eschatological meaning

(d) Dedication to the will of God: Jesus says: 'But not what I will but what you (will')

To understand this statement we must look at the idea of 'will of God'.[19]

We can slip without knowing into a false idea of the will of God as a mysterious force that more or less constrains intelligence and feelings, and may even thwart them. It can be seen as a command that I must carry out even though I do not agree with it. One cannot deny that there has been a current of spirituality that has turned the will of God into something capricious and menacing, something that one cannot escape and that will strike in one's unguarded moments.

The biblical notion of the will of God bears little resemblance to this. The translation goes back to the Greek words *thèlèma* or *eudokia*. Both words are used to translate the Hebrew *rasôn* (or sometimes *hps*). The Hebrew words signify the idea of longing, love and joy. The idea of being in love and sexual attraction are denoted by the same words. Thus the love (will of God) rests upon the people that God chose for himself in his good pleasure. In Is 62:3-5 the idea of Will of God signifies the pleasure the Lord takes in his people and the joy he has in them.

The fullness of that love rests on Jesus. He is the one in whom God delights. He heard this at the baptism and transfiguration (9:2-7) The Father bears witness that the fullness of his will - in the sense of love, longing and delight - rests upon his well-beloved son. So Jesus himself is the place where God reveals himself, the human being in whom the *thèlèma*, the yearning, the love and the will of the Father, are made plain. All that happens is in accord with the Father's will and that will is worked out even in the darkest of situations. Jesus is coming to realise that his mission will end in failure and violence. Yet even in this God's loving purpose will be realised and Jesus gives himself over to the will of God which will be realised in spite of sorrow and death. In Chapter 11 Jesus spoke of God being able to do all things and that he would do whatever he was asked for in prayer (11:22-27). In the Gethsemane prayer we see that the idea of 'will of God' comes into play and prayer must be made according to the loving purpose of God. This is how Jesus prays.

* * * * *

The readers of Mark will be led to realise, when they read of the disciples' sleep, that they are the ones who actually keep vigil with Jesus as he prays. The original readers of Mark who had experienced persecution were being led in the spirit of Jesus to face their own hour of darkness with the same hope in God's purpose. In our time, as we share Jesus' darkness, we are being led to see that even in our darkest moments, when we feel alone, we can meet God and realise his will (ie His loving purpose).

109

In the final prayer of Jesus we hear his anguished cry on the cross (15:34). This is the prayer of one who has lost all sense of divine presence. However, in the actual context of the psalms of lament, as we saw, there is also an element of trust involved. The psalmist believes that when we pray in this way, God responds and comes to the one who is so troubled. The words of Jesus are taken from the beginning of Ps 22, and this forms one of the psalms of lament. Taken in this context Jesus' prayer is not an isolated cry of utter despair but is charged with the meaning of the whole psalm from which these words are taken. He knows his Father will hear his cry and that through this dark hour he will be vindicated. Luke brings out the idea of Jesus abandoning himself to the Father more so than Mark (cf. Lk23:46). There Jesus says, 'Father, into your hands I commit my spirit.' This idea is implicitly present in Mark's use of Ps 22.

Christ drew near to all human beings and, in a particular way, to their sufferings. His own body on the cross expressed his mysterious but truly redeeming presence to those who suffer. Pascal reflected on this and he said. 'He is in agony to the end of the world'! [20] Here Pascal articulated the crucified Christ's enduring presence in the mystery of all human suffering. Even in our darkest moments we are no longer alone.

At the cross of Jesus the centurion heard his prayer and realised that there was something special about Jesus. He said, 'In truth this man was Son of God.' (15:39). This was the beginning of others' realisation of Jesus' uniqueness and his special relationship with God.

Gethsemane and My Prayer

John O'Donohue [21] muses on the person called Jesus. He wonders what it would be like to know Jesus. He says that it would be fascinating to have the possibility of excavating the inner landscape of Jesus' solitude. Could he glimpse the lonely consequences his choice would have? He would become the suffering servant of life's most merciless negativity. But he would achieve a beauty beyond conventional understanding to which poets, artists and mystics have responded for two millennia.

Jesus would not enter his destiny as a victim or accidental martyr. O'Donohue goes on to say that through choice, Christ gathered into the circle of his heart the pain of the world. He was overcome with doubt and fear in the garden. Here the anguish of human desolation reached out for divine consolation. All that was heard was the silence of the heavens. No voice was heard this time. His friends betrayed and abandoned him. Christ explores the endless heart of loss with such gentle and vulnerable courage.

He exhibited unconditional love. When this love produced rejection, he did not deny his love and showed how defenceless this love in fact was when he was rejected. His defencelessness led him to his agony in Gethsemane and ultimately to his death on the cross. His offer of love was not withdrawn and reconciliation with God was held out to those who would share in this love. His resurrection would show that Jesus was vindicated. Here is where I see the importance of Jesus' prayer in Gethsemane. It was in his prayer that he gained strength to continue offering defenceless love - in the face of failure and God's silence. I have, as I said, often drawn strength in my own journey of life from the prayer-scene of Gethsemane.

The first thing the prayer of Jesus led me to question was the image of God that I had. The significance of Jesus' address to God was important in my journey. Jesus' calling of God, '*Abba*', strongly suggests that this was the language of experience rather than a formal address. It was his experience of God that found expression in the *Abba*-prayer. Rom 8:15 and Gal 4:6 witness to the fact that Jesus did not keep the '*Abba*' form of address to himself but encouraged those of his new family to address God in this way.

For the moment in Gethsemane God remains silent. In the darkness of many people's lives, too, I hear so many say that

God is silent. Atheism becomes an option. In my own life I once had a picture of God as somehow distant and unmoved by our tears. JB Phillips and Harry Williams speak in their own way of how they projected onto God a figure of a demanding, perfectionist father. Many people suffer from the same idea of God.

I found relief from my negative picture of God in contemplating the love and trust of Jesus as he called God's name into the silence. He knew that his prayer would be heard, but maybe not in the way he hoped. This god, *Abba*, was the God of the Old-Testament. In the reflections of Abraham Heschel [22] and the God of the Old Testament I find myself able to move on from my primitive picture of God. God created men and women in his own likeness (Gen 1:26-27) and Heschel goes on to analyse the relationship between God and his creation.

When we examine the idea of God in the Old Testament, we learn that His transcendence is not to be interpreted as sheer 'otherness', as distance or inaccessibility. On the contrary - he is near to his creation and cares for it. Heschel introduces his concept of the pathos of God to help us understand God's relationship to his creation and his people. In the biblical tradition God is not isolated in a transcendental realm, but is present and manifests himself in the world. He is not to be understood as detached and unaffected by what goes on in the world. 'God does not stand outside the range of human suffering and sorrow. He is personally involved in, even stirred by, the conduct and fate of man.' [23] This pathos or deep feeling on the part of God is linked to the phenomenon of prophecy that was so characteristic of Israel's religion. The prophet is stirred by an infinite concern for the divine concern. Sympathy is the essential mode in which he responds to the situation. [24] In this the prophet is both a 'partner' and 'associate' of God. [25] There is intimacy and distinction between God and his prophets.

The objection that could be made in that this pathos of which Heschel wrote is a from of anthropomorphism which clung to

Israel's idea of God. John Macquarrie answers this objection by referring to the place of feelings or emotions in the life of a human being. [26]

He points out that many of us have a low estimate of the place of feelings and emotions in our lives. It is a long journey from the head to the heart. However, if men and women are indeed made in the image of God, it is not just in their rationality or capacity for thought that they reflect God but in the entire range of spirit, and because of this the place of feelings cannot be excluded. If there really is a mysterious affinity between the divine and the human, then in some way the emotional life in the person must point to an analogue in God. It is to this God that Jesus prays. For a brief while he remains silent but the author of the letter to the Hebrews assures us: 'During his life on earth he offered up prayer and entreaty, aloud and in silent tears to the one who had the power to save him out of death and he submitted so humbly his prayer was heard.' (Hebrew 5:7). Even though God remained silent, Jesus was in the end vindicated and called those in darkness to walk with him to a new beginning. God's will or his love had the ultimate say.

This leads me to consider how I view my prayer and my relationship with this God. John O'Donohue says that one of the most beautiful images is that of the human person at prayer. When the persons gather themselves before the Divine, a stillness deepens. [27] He goes on to describe the rich beauty that is to be found all around us, but says we live in a time when it is more fashionable to see people and things in their darkest colours. If we concentrate exclusively on the negative side we begin to feel powerless and victimised. In the silence of our prayer we shall be able to sense the smile of a joyful God who, despite all the chaos and imperfection, ultimately shelters everything. Prayer is the art of being present to God. [28]

This view is one the person who suffers from depression illness or rejection can feel isolated from. The world and people appear in their darkest shades. The Indian poet Kabir once said: 'If thy soul is a stranger to thee, the whole world becomes unfriendly.' When we do not feel at home in ourselves then our perception of God, people and the world around us is clouded and we feel isolated and alone.

In the dark hours of loneliness it is hard to be present to God who so often appears silent and distant.

* * * * *

Henri JM Nouwen also offers a definition of prayer. [29] He says the best formulation of the idea of prayer of the heart is found in the words of the Russian mystic Theophan, the recluse, who says: 'To pray is to descend with the mind into the heart and there to stand before the face of the Lord, ever present, all-seeing within you.' Prayer is being present to God, standing in his presence with the mind in the heart; that is, at that point of our being where there are no divisions or distinctions and where we are totally one. There God's spirit dwells and our encounter takes place. Heart speaks to heart in love.

The word 'heart' is used in its biblical sense. [30] In our milieu it refers to the seat of the sentimental life. However, the word in its Jewish-Christian sense refers to the source of all physical, emotional, intellectual, volitional and moral energies. It is also the seat of the will: it makes plans and comes to good decisions. The prayer of the heart is a prayer that directs itself to God from the centre of the person and this affects the whole of our humanness.

I remember hearing about the advice Meister Eckhart gave. He was talking to someone who felt they had lost God. He recommended that the person return to where thy last knew God and they would find Him there. Theophan's definition of prayer is truly useful but I have often found that when I pray God is silent and I am not aware of His presence, then I love to return to the place I have met Him before and learn that He is always present, even in his silence.

114

The time I return to is a time in my life when I was ill. This was a time when I suffered a number of traumatic experiences and God appeared to be absent. The God of Theophan or of O'Donohue's prayer seemed far away. The prayer of Jesus in Gethsemane found echoes in my life. I was severely depressed and my physical health began to fail. I was living in Rome at the time. One day when I was at my weakest I fell asleep and when I awoke I found myself strangely at peace. My recovery began at that moment.

What I did not realise at that time was that there were two friends of mine in Assisi. On the morning I was at my weakest they went to mass in the Basilica of Saint Francis. There they had an intuition that I wasn't well. They felt moved to pray for me. They prayed many prayers until they felt spun out. One of my friends heard an interior voice asking what prayer could she say. The only answer she could give was to give all her love to the prayer. She had arrived at prayer of the heart without knowing it. After this both of them offered up all the love they had in their hearts. They heard an inner voice telling them their prayer was heard. It was at this time that I awoke from my sleep and began my journey on the road to healing. In their love I saw a reflection of God's love. He had led them to prayer of the heart and to share their love, in prayer. I had felt God was absent yet at that moment I came to realise that He was not absent, that even in my darkest moments I was not alone. Jesus' agony in Gethsemane and on the cross pointed me in this direction. The prayer and love of friends was a reflection of God's love for me and for humankind. As Pascal pointed out [31], the suffering Christ is present in the midst of all human suffering and the love of God reaches out to that person even though for a time He appears silent. It was thanks to this lesson that I learnt to appreciate the insights of people like O'Donohue and Theophan the Recluse.

One final teacher who guides me in prayer is the figure of Saint Francis. He is helpful to me in seeing how to bring prayer into the hubbub of daily living. He often contemplated the love of God revealed in Jesus the Christ and he, too, became infused with the same love that was in Jesus. We are told:

'This was also shown to blessed Francis when he was enraptured in contemplation on the high mountain ... There he passed over into God through contemplative rapture and was established as an example of perfect contemplation, just as he had been previously of action. And so, like another Jacob and Israel, through him God might invite all other truly spiritual men to this kind of passing over and ecstasy of mind, more by example than by word.' (Bonaventure, Journey of the Mind into God, 7:3)

Contemplation is where the heart loves God and is loved by God in return. Francis combined action and contemplation and showed that both forms of life can belong together. Thomas of Celano, another biographer of Saint Francis, tells us of Saint Francis'prayer. He speaks of Francis 'not so much praying as becoming himself a prayer'. (2 Cel 95) This helps me see how Francis could pray always. He was always present to the Father as Jesus was; his life flowed from that loving union. It also helps me make sense of a passage we looked at concerning Jesus' prayer. It is the part of Mark 9:16-29 where a distracted father had bought his son to the disciples, who failed to cure him. From Mark's description of the boy it appears he was suffering from epilepsy. Jesus heals the boy. Later the disciples ask him why they were unable to cure the boy. Jesus answers then that it is only by prayer that a cure can take place, in this case. Yet in the passage there is no mention of Jesus formally saying any prayer. Mark leaves us with no explanation of this, thus enabling the readers to search for a meaning themselves. I see the key to an understanding of this passage in St Francis. He was present to God as Jesus was to the Father. He became prayer just as Jesus had, and because Jesus was prayer itself, he was able to bring peace to the spirit of the boy. The disciples had not learnt the art of prayer and they could not mediate peace to the boy.

In Saint Francis I see how to begin to pray always. Also, in the *Diary of a Russian Pilgrim* we hear of the Jesus prayer which helps us enter into our hearts and gently call out the Jesus prayer which helps us to enter the very presence of God Himself. When we learn to remain present to God in whatever way we choose then the channels for compassionate living become open to us.

Compassion and Prayer

One of the fruits of prayer is to see that just as we are held and loved by God, so too are all our brothers and sisters. The love God has for them can be mediated through the human story of our interactions. Compassion is one of the fruits of prayer - in our struggles and failures we learn compassion for our brothers and sisters. This message was brought home very much to me by the story of Benedetta Bianchi Porro. Her story is a living commentary on what I have just said.

The outline of her lifestory goes as follows. She was born in 1936 in Dovadola near Forli and died on the 23 January 1964 in Sirmione near Brescia. Stricken with polio when she was a few months old, she could attend school only intermittently throughout her childhood. Yet she had a vision of being able to help those who found life as difficult as it had been for her, and she enrolled at the medical school of the University of Milan. By now she was also growing deaf, which caused her many humiliations, but she tenaciously persisted in her studies. At times she could become very dispirited. She shared some of her negative thoughts, including occasional thoughts of suicide, with her friend Maria Grazia.

At one time in her university career she encountered severe humiliation at the hands of one of her lecturers. He was not in the least bit sensitive to her predicament. When she asked him, during an exam, to repeat a question, he refused, pouring scorn on her and asking her whoever heard of a deaf doctor. She retreated hurt from the exam, excusing herself for having caused offence. The lecturer had abused his power and Benedetta's fellow-students were angry. Their complaints were heard and Benedetta was allowed to re-sit the exam.

This was not the end of Benedetta's *via crucis*. Deafness was followed by blindness and then by total paralysis. She was diagnosed as having Recklinghausen's disease which would see her suffering still more. However, this was not the end of the story of Benedetta. She was full of love and she made many friends who shared her moments of darkness with her. They found joy and love being with her. She became an ambassador of the Gospel by her life and voluminous correspondence dictated to her mother. [32]

How did her love develop? The answer lies in the prayerful attitude she developed in her suffering. Oscar Wilde once wrote:

'How else but through a broken heart.
May Lord Christ enter in?' (*The Ballad of Reading Gaol*)

Benedetta's heart and body were broken, but her darkness did not overcome her. She shared Christ's lonely vigil of Gethsemane. She too was sustained by her prayer. She came to believe that 'great souls are born out of loneliness'.[33] Where did she learn to pray her illness and live such a compassionate life? The answer lies in the many friends she made who shared her darkness. She found friendship life-giving.

One of the friends who was with Benedetta was a Don Elios Mori. [34] This humble priest was much loved by Benedetta and he shared her spiritual journey with her as she became increasingly weaker. In his letter of 9 September 1959, we find him offering a form of guidance as to how she should pray and live her illness. He begins by telling her not to ask where God is. He tells her that God is beside her all the time. He is present in her sufferings and she can turn to meet him there. He goes on to tell her that God can understand her well. He tells her that Jesus on the cross did not know what to do or say. The cross, however, was the most valid moment

118

of his life. He tells her that her cross resembles that of Christ, it is a continuation of Christ's suffering. Don Elios' words echo the words of the letter to the Colossians. 'In my flesh I am completing what is lacking in Christ's afflictions for the sake of his body, that is, the church.' (Col 1:24).

Don Elios goes on to tell her that he would remember her every day as he said mass. He describes how he will pray for her, offering her sufferings into the hands of God. He counsels her not to be worried when she does not know how to pray or what to say in prayer. He tells her that on one's cross it is not possible to speak fine discourses. He recounts how on Calvary Jesus could just say a few words while Mary his mother could only remain silent in her lonely vigil with her son. He tells her to do as they do, to present herself into the hands of God as she is. When she can't find words, she should remember that the Lord knows what is in her heart.

She is not to be surprised if at times she feels she is losing heart or feels a sense of rebellion welling up inside her which she cannot hold back. Sometimes this sense of rebellion just explodes within us. Don Elios touches on something important here. Many people grow weary of the tormented struggles in their minds when they are struck by some traumatic event. I know this from my own experience and the experience of others who have come across my path. When lost in a world of doubt and darkness anger can rise to the surface; anger against God, against other people and against life. Many of us are afraid of our anger and try to suppress it. We feel somehow unworthy. Don Elios comforts Benedetta when she has to face her moments of rebellion by telling her that this rebellion can't bring us far from God. Even in rebellion he tells her to trust in Jesus and Mary; beyond the clouds there is always sunshine.

He tells her of the compassion of Jesus. He discovered in his experience what Benedetta discovered in her darkest moments. He was able to be close to her because he too had suffered. There Don Elios echoes the author of the letter to the Hebrews who said: 'We have one [high-priest] who has been tested as we are.' (Heb 4:15).

119

He goes on to tell Benedetta not to desire death but life. He tells her to allow God to lead her into living as he wants. He touches on the mystery of suffering. He tells us that the cross of Jesus, the sadness of Mary and the pain of all Christians form the greatest treasure that the world has. Later, in another context, Harry Williams, when speaking of the pain of his depression which could not be lifted totally, would say: 'On the deepest level of reality it [breakdown] could be recognised as an invitation to share to some small degree in the sufferings of Christ, that is, in the birth-pangs of creation by means of which God's one creative act accomplishes its perfect and glorious conclusion. In other words when one had done everything in one's power to rid oneself of one's disabilities, those that remained could be used as a prayer for others and thus be a channel for God's life-giving love.' [35] Benedetta would live this out in a pre-eminent way. Don Elios reminds her that in her sufferings she is close to Jesus. By implication her illness and loneliness is where she meets Jesus and shares his sufferings, allowing herself to be a channel of God's grace.

He goes on to tell her that her wheelchair; her bed of pain, is where she offers herself into the hands of God, just as the host is offered in the altar. He tells her not to believe she has little faith but to continue her prayer - offering of herself in the face of doubt. God sees the heart of the person who prays. She, too, learnt the prayer of the heart.

In another letter sent the following year, 1960, Don Elios continues his sharing in Benedetta's spiritual journey. He speaks of the emotional storms she undergoes, telling her to always return to God's embrace. He tells her it is love that gives value to everything, especially her sufferings. If she feels she has committed any offence against love then he tells her to compensate for this by loving even more. If she feels she is losing courage then she is to hasten to reach out in love to Jesus and Mary. Her spiritual courage comes from God and he tells her to go to meet him in her hours of darkness. He tells her she is not in this world to suffer but to love. Because she is so ill and troubled she is actually very close to the source of love, God himself.

In their correspondence Don Elios taught Benedetta how to pray her loneliness. He taught her always to be present to God even when afflicted by a sense of his absence. He taught her to relate to the sufferings of Christ. He taught her the value of silence and solitude. He shared with her her journey of dryness, of rebellion, of love and of abandoment to God's will, as Christ had done. He taught her to meet God in her illness and feelings of loneliness. She was no longer alone. It was in this way that Benedetta was present to God. It was in this spirit that she prayed.

The fruits of Benedetta's prayers can best be gleaned by us from her correspondence. There she shows love to those who feel lonely and lost. One of the best examples of this is a correspondence she built up with a student called Natalino Dioloti who suffered from spinal difficulties. He poured out his anger, bitterness and despair in a letter he wrote to an Italian magazine, in a desperate search for help. He signed his letter "on behalf of the victims." Benedetta's love made her many friends and they told her of Natalino. This was the reply Benedetta wrote to the lonely Natalino. [36]

Sirmione 1963

Dear Natalino
There's a letter of yours in Epoca. My mother read it to me by touching hands. I'm deaf and blind, so we have to do things the hard way.

Like you, I am twenty-six and have been sick for some time. A disease shrivelled me up just as I was about to complete long years of study. I was about to graduate in medicine in Milan. I had been complaining of deafness for some time but even the doctors didn't believe me at first. So I plunged ahead with my studies, which I was absolutely crazy about, even though I knew the doctors were wrong. I was only seventeen when I started at university.

Then my sickness stopped me cold, just when I'd nearly finished my studies. I was taking my last exam. And the only thing my 'almost-degree' was good for self-diagnosis, since until then no one had been able to decide what was the matter with me.

Until three months ago I still had fairly good vision. But now all is dark. I'm not hopeless here on my Calvary, though. I know Jesus is waiting for me at the end of the road.

To begin with I lived in a big chair, but now I have to stay in bed. Here I have found a wisdom greater than that of mankind. I've found that there is a God, and that he is love, faithfulness, joy and certainly, even to the end of the world.

Before long I shall be no more than a name. But my spirit will live on here among my family, and among those who suffer; even I shall not have suffered in vain.

Natalino, don't feel alone. Never. Go calmly on down the path of time, and you'll receive light, truth. This is the road where there's really a righteousness, not the righteousness of men and women but the righteousness that God alone can give.

My days are not easy. They're hard. But they're sweet because Jesus is with me in my suffering. He comforts me in my loneliness and lightens my darkness.

He smiles at me and lets me work with him. So long, Natalino. Life is short. It passes in a flash. Life is a very short bridge: dangerous for people who want to get all the enjoyment out of it they can, but safe for those who cooperate with Jesus to reach our Homeland.

All love,
Your sister in Christ
Benedetta

It is not easy to speak like this when one is in pain but Benedetta had placed her suffering in the hands of love. The fruit of her prayer was love and compassion. This compassion led Natalino on a journey of self acceptance. He was deeply touched by the love and compassion Benedetta had shown him.

Benedetta is the one who prayed through her darkness. She shared Jesus' lonely hour in Gethsemane, and like him she abandoned herself to the loving purpose and will of God. Her giving of herself in love in the face of darkness is something that stays with me as I struggle through my own darkness and learn to pray therein. Benedetta says:

'As for myself, I live the way I always did and feel perfectly fulfilled ... and I think of it as a miracle and I should be able to raise a hymn of praise to the One who has given me life ... At times I wonder whether I am not one of those creatures to whom much has been given and of whom much will be asked.'

And again:

'In the sorrow of my blindness, in the deep darkness of my loneliness, I have tried, willing myself to be serene, to make my sorrow blossom; and thus I seek the humble will to succeed in being as God wishes me: very tiny, as I sincerely believe myself to be, when I manage to see his stupendous grandeur in the dark night of my weary days.'

NOTES ON CHAPTER 5

1. A Stock, *The Way in the Wilderness* (Collegeville, MN: Liturgical Press, 1969) p89.
2. cf A Stock, op. cit, p.73ff, and U Mauser, *Christ in the Wilderness* (Naperville. Alec R. Allensen, Inc,. 1963) p105-108.
3. R Ellsberg, *Charles De Foucauld: Selected Writings* (New York: Orbis 1999) p.24
4. MA Tolbert, *Sowing the Gospel: Mark's World in Literary Historical Perspective* (Minneapolis Fortress Press 1989) p138
5. John Dominic Crossan, *The Historical Jesus: The Life of a Mediteranean Jewish Peasant* (San Francisco Harper 1991), p346
6. R Fowler, *Let the Reader Understand* (Minneapolis Fortress Press 1991) p68
7. J Gilbert, 'La Prière de Jesus' (Mc 14:32-42) in *L'Experience de la Prière dans les Grands Réligions*, H Limet and J Ries (eds.) (Louvain la Neuve: Centre d'Histoire des Réligions, 1980, p261-273 art 265.

8. The most concise treatment of his argument concerning '*Abba*' is found in J Jeremias *The Central Message of the New Testament* (London: SCM, 1965), p.9-30. So also his '*Abba*' (Gottingen: Vandenhoeck and, Ruprecht, 1966), p15-67.

9. J Jeremias Central Message, (n(8)), p.16.

10. J Ashton, '*Abba*', ABD i 7-8   art   7.

11. JA Fitzmyer, '*Abba* and Jesus' Relation to God' in *A Cause de l'Evangile*, Lectio Divina 123 (Paris: Editions du Cerf, 1988) p.15-38 at p28

12. As found in G Vernes, *The Dead Sea Scrolls in English* (Hamondsworth: Penguin Books, 3rd edition 1987) p192

13. E Underhill, *The Mystic Way* (London: J.M. Dent, 1914) p89.

14. J Gilbert, n(7) p267

15. CEB Cranfield, The Cup Metaphor in Mark XIV, 36 and Parallels, Expasitory Times 59 (1947-1948), p.137-138 at 137

16. AT Hanson, *The Wrath of the Lamb* (London: SPCK, 1957) p27-39

17. RE Brown, *The Death of the Messiah* (London: Chapman, 1993), 1.169

18. R le Deaut, *Goûter le Calice de la Mort*, Biblica 43 (1962), p82-86.

19. For this discussion on the will of God I use Andre Louf's *Teach Us to Pray* (London: Darton, Longman, Todd, 1974) p28f

20. Listed as 'Pensée 552' in WF Trotter's translation (New York: E.P Dutton, 1958).

21. J O'Donohue, *Eternal Echoes* (London: Bantam Press, 1998) p.170

22. AJ Heschel, *The Prophets* (London: Harper, Row, 1962).

23. Ibid, p224

24. Ibid, p308

25. Ibid, p25

26. J Macquarries, *Jesus Christ in Modern Thought* (London: SCM, 1990) p31

27. J O'Donohue, n(21), p188-190

28. Ibid, p199

29. HJM Nouwen, *The Way of the Heart* (London: Darton, Longman, Todd, 1999 edition) p65

30. See J Behm, *Kardia* (TDNT3) pp606-609

31. See n(20).

32. Her correspondence was collected by Anna Maria Coppelli and published as *Oltre Il Silenzio* (Amici di Benedetta: Forli, 1972).

33. As quoted by Lorenzo da Fara, *Benedetta Biunchi Porro*, (Padova: Caroccio, 1986) p110.

34. See *Oltre Il Silenzio*, p94ff.

35. HA Williams, *Someday I'll Find You* (London: Fount Paperbacks, 1984) pp2-67f

36. See n(32), p94f

37. As quoted by Calo Carretto, *Why, O Lord?* (London: D.L.T., 1986), p104.

CHAPTER 6

THE SPIRITUALITY OF IMPERFECTION:
THE DISCIPLES

The readers who came to Mark's account of Gethsemane find that Mark initiates a conversation with them. In reading this scene the reader shares in the passion of Jesus. When the scene turns to look at the disciples, unbelievably, we find that they are sleeping. The one who shares Jesus' lonely vigil in the garden is the reader. This time there is no heavenly voice - all is silent. Mark uses the disciples to highlight this. Meditating on the disciples in Mark leads the readers to ask questions about themselves and how they cope.

'They came to a plot of land called Gethsemane, and he said to his disciples, "Stay here while I pray." Then he took Peter and James and John with him. (Mk 14:32f)

Gethsemane itself means 'oil press'.[1] This is linked with the idea of Gethsemane being at the Mount of Olives. Jesus is now coming face to face with the onrush of his approaching fate. He takes Peter, James and John with him perhaps so that he will not be totally alone in his hour of need. Peter, James and John seem to form an inner group amongst the twelve. They are together with Jesus at the raising of Jairus' daughter (5:35-43), the transfiguration (9:2-7), and with Andrew at the so-called eschatological discourse (Chapter 13).

'He came back and found them sleeping, and he said to Peter, "Simon, are you asleep? Had you not the strength to stay awake one hour? Stay awake and pray not to be put to the test. The spirit is willing enough, but human nature is weak." Again he went away and prayed, saying the same words. And once more he came back and found them sleeping, their eyes were so heavy; and they could find no answer for him. He came back a third time and said to them, "You can sleep on now and have your rest. It is all over. The hour has come. Now the Son of man is to be betrayed into the hands of sinners. Get up! Let us go! My betrayer is not far away." ' (14:37-42).

Immediately after Jesus prayed he came back to those he had asked to be with him, but he found them asleep. The sleep of the disciples is a symbol in Mark's gospel of their incomprehension of the real character of Jesus' vocation as God's suffering servant (cf Is 52:13-53:12). Now he asks them to stay awake and pray so that they will be able to face the oncoming hours of trial. This going and coming is repeated twice more. Each time the disciples fall asleep. Their insensitivity is highlighted by Mark.

Jesus tells them, 'The Spirit is willing, but human nature is weak.' (14:38) DM Stanley says that Jesus here speaks of his own immediate experiences as a human being. [2] He is indeed willing in the truest part of himself which Mark designates as his spirit, yet at the same time he feels the weight of his human nature as he struggles to accept God's will. Eventually Jesus comes to accept his fate and at the end of the scene his composure returns. He says to the disciples, 'Get up! Let us go! My betrayer is not far away'. Jesus had been strengthened in his prayer to face his betrayer, but the disciples have not prayed and they are overwhelmed when Judas and those who wish to arrest Jesus appear. We are told 'and they all deserted him and ran away'. (14:50).

Another thing to note in the dialogue between Jesus and his disciples is that he addressed Peter as 'Simon'. He is no longer Peter, the rock, but Simon. There was a breakdown in the relationship between Peter and Jesus. Peter would even deny he knew Jesus (14:66-72).

To understand what Mark is doing in this scene it is necessary to see this passage in relationship to the other passages of Mark that concern the disciples and see the way Mark involves the reader in his narrative and how the text leads

127

the reader to question their own attitudes. I now turn my attention to this question.

What was Mark trying to say? [3]

Mark gives us a single unified story in his gospel. Jesus is the central figure in the story and he gathers round him a group of disciples. The Greek work for disciple is *mathetes*. [4] Jesus called men and women to follow after him (*akoulouthein*). A *mathetes* was someone who learnt. Unlike the disciple in Rabbinic Judaism, the disciples of Jesus did not choose him, rather, he chose them (1:17, 2:14). In Mk 3:13-13 Jesus called those he desired to be with him, so that he might send them out to preach. Among those who were asked to follow him were the outsiders and those who had been ostracized, the tax-collectors and sinners (Mk 2:15). In the 'way' section of Mark, where Jesus begins to journey towards Jerusalem (Mk 8:34-10:52), Mark provides an extended instruction on discipleship. The way of Jesus involves taking up one's cross and following him (8:34-35).

Now I come to ask what was Mark's purpose in his portrayal of the disciples? We have seen them sleep in Gethsemane; but that is just the culmination of the disciples' incomprehension of Jesus. Mark has pointed out long before the strained relations between Jesus and the twelve.

The brief portraits of people in Mark are like pen and ink sketches in which the artist with just a few strokes has suggested some forms, relying on the viewer to fill in the rest. This selective emphasis of the artist can help us see the subject in a new way. In Mark we can see the way he emphasised things and suggests a negative or positive evaluation of the disciples' actions. This is part of the ongoing dialogue that exists between author and audience. The author wishes to emphasise certain points. For instance in Mark certain aspects of the story are highlighted by repetition. These include elements in a single scene (Jesus returns three times to the disciples in Gethsemane, Peter denies Jesus three times) and repetition of statements in a single scene (Jesus feeds a multitude twice, followed in both cases by a boat scene which reveals the disciples' lack of understanding).

In the gospel of Mark it is Jesus who is the central character. We already know from 1:1 who Jesus is and we look at the way he reveals himself in the gospel. We judge the words and actions of others in the light of Jesus. Our guide to the evaluation of the disciples arises from our analysis of the shifting relationship between Jesus and his disciples. Just as we evaluate events in ordinary life, so Mark expects us when we enter his world to arrive at our own evaluation. The characters in his story to whom we are attracted or repelled can lead us to changes in our behaviour and self-understanding. There is a natural connection between the story and our experience of life.

Assuming that the majority of the first readers of the Gospel were Christians, they would relate more easily and immediately to characters in the story who respond positively to Jesus. The disciples, including the twelve, are the characters who seem most to fulfil this role. Tannehill [5] believes that Mark would have anticipated this response by his readers. He composed his story so as to make use of this initial tendency to identify with the disciples in order to speak indirectly to the reader through the disciples' story. In so doing he at first reinforces the positive view of the disciples. Then gradually he reveals the inadequacy of the disciples' response to Jesus, presents the disciples in conflict with Jesus on important issues, and finally shows the disciples as failures. The surprising negative development gradually requires the readers to distance themselves from the disciples' side to the side of Jesus. Yet, all the time, there remains some identification between the readers and the disciples. This tension between identification and repulsion can lead the sensitive readers to self-criticism and repentance. The readers can see their own failures and through the story of Mark can be led to the side of Jesus, there to find reconciliation and healing. We are left with a choice when we enter the world of Mark, a choice represented by the differing ways of Jesus and his disciples.

Beginning in 8:31 Jesus clearly announces his coming passion and resurrection, and Mark brings out the disciples' reaction with care. The passion of Jesus presents discipleship in its sharpest form. Following the crucified Jesus means taking up the cross oneself (8:34). It means becoming the servant of all as Jesus himself was a servant (10:44-45). These are not demands that disappear after Easter, nor do they become easy to fulfil. Living with all that life throws at us can be difficult; those who have suffered mental anguish know how hard it is to find a faith-response. Those who heard Jesus' message first failed to follow him, and an indication of further failure by Jesus' followers (16:8) comes immediately after the resurrection message at the tomb. In telling us a story of the past, Mark manages to speak to us in the present.

Wolfgang Iser [6] looked at the issue of the role of negative portrayal of people in a narrative. 'Negation' in a story impels the readers to seek a counter-balance elsewhere than in the world immediately familiar to them. The readers are forced to take an active part in the composition of the story's meaning for them. The negativity in a story induces the readers to ponder what went wrong and imagine an alternative. This negation of the expected encourages 'the reader's production of the meaning of a text." [7]

The strong negative aspect of the disciples' story in Mark functions in a similar way, moving the readers to ponder how those called by Jesus could go so far astray and what is required if they are to escape a similar failure. [8] Jesus represents the positive alternative to the failure of the disciples and we, in coping with our own negativity, are encouraged to walk the path he walked leading from

Gethsemane to Calvary, to our resurrection as transformed people.

Mark's Story of the Disciples

We now look at the principal episodes in Mark's story of the disciples. Jesus, just after he begins his preaching, calls four disciples who will later take their place among the twelve (1:16-20). Jesus' command to follow him becomes the norm by which we, the readers, can judge the behaviour of the disciples. At this point the disciples obey the command. Later on Jesus will call them again to follow him on the road to the cross (8:34), but this time he is met by incomprehension. In 3:13-19 Jesus selected twelve for a special relationship with him and for a special responsibility. They are Jesus' choice and they work with him by sharing in the works of preaching and exorcism which Jesus had been doing. Here a jarring note is struck when Judas is identified as the one close to Jesus who would violate his trust and betray him (3:19). In 6:7-13 the twelve are actually sent on a mission to perform the works of Jesus. There is no indication that they fail, but they do encounter opposition. Overall in the earlier chapters of Mark, the picture of the disciples is largely positive.

In 2:14-28 Jesus, together with the disciples, faces the criticism of the Scribes and Pharisees while he defends himself and his disciples. Jesus stands together with them. By 7:14-23 this early unity has become strained. Jesus has been speaking about clean and unclean foods but the disciples do not understand.

In 3:20-35 the Scribes' opposition to Jesus is emphasized. Jesus' family are disturbed by what is happening to him and they too are seen in opposition to Jesus. In 3:31-35 'those around Jesus', his new family, are contrasted with his natural family. 'Those around him' are those who do the will of God; the person who does this is 'my father, and sister and mother' (3:35). The phrase 'those around him', his family, is carried over to 4:10, where the twelve are associated with this group. Here the mystery of the kingdom is given to those about Jesus, while those outside do not see. This comes in the context of Jesus explaining the meaning of the parable of the sower. Thus far the readers can identify with the positive qualities the disciples have. We have high expectations of those about Jesus at this stage, but what we have in view is the literary technique which encourages us to contemplate one possibility so that we shall feel more sharply the opposite development when it arrives. Jesus' authoritative statement, 'He told them "to you is granted the secret of the Kingdom of God, but to those outside everything comes in parables' "(4:11), will serve as a norm by which the response of the disciples will be measured (see 8:17-18). This involves the readers at the level of their decision-making and faith response.

When we look back at Mark from the standpoint of the end of the gospel we see the suggestion of the possibility of a negative development in the disciples' story. Firstly the hearing of the word is presented as a problem (4:1-9). The world does not always fall on good ground and it does not always bear fruit when it has begun to grow. There is a mention of the seed falling on rocky ground (4:5). The Greek word for 'rocky' (*petrodes*) involves a play on Peter's name (*Petros*).

There is a hint here that Peter might not receive the word as meant by Jesus. When Jesus explains why he spoke in parables (4:12), the impression given is that the disciples are the 'inside', but as the story develops we see that the word did not take root in the disciples. Gradually we, the readers, begin to realize that it is the reader who is on the inside. We become involved with Jesus.

Jesus' teaching in Mark 4 is followed by the stilling of the storm at sea. The disciples are criticized for their cowardice and lack of faith (4:40) and appear not to understand Jesus (4:41). In 6:35-41, we see the disciples again facing a storm at sea and once again they are afraid. Jesus comes to them on the water and the storm is calmed. The disciples in this episode seem to have forgotten totally the stilling of the storm at sea in 4:35-41.

The call of the four disciples (1:16-20), the choice of the twelve (3:13-19) and the mission of the twelve (6:7-13,30) appear to be linked scenes which reinforce and develop a particular view of the twelve. This compositional technique of linking scenes by repeating and thereby emphasizing and developing a set of motifs reappears in the three boat scenes in the first half of Mark. These three boat scenes - the stilling of the storm at sea, (4:35-41), the encounter with Jesus on the water (6:45-52) and the discussion with Jesus in a boat (8:14-21) - isolate Jesus and his disciples from the crowds by the setting of the scene, and highlight the disciples' attitude. The first two boat scenes, as we have seen, show the disciples' difficulty with the sea, Jesus' miraculous power and the disciples' fear and incomprehension. The third is not a miracle story but it is linked to the second by references to Jesus feeding a multitude, and by presenting in a most emphatic way the disciples' failure to understand.

'The disciples had forgotten to take any bread and they had only one loaf with them in the boat. Then he gave them this warning: "Keep your eyes open; look out for the yeast of the Pharisees and the yeast of Herod". And they said to one another, "It is because we have no bread." And Jesus knew it, and he said to them, "Are your minds closed? Have you eyes and do not see, ears and do not hear? Or do you not remember? When I broke the five loaves for the five thousand, how many baskets full of scraps did you collect?" They answered, "Twelve." "And when I broke the seven loaves for the four thousand, how many baskets full of scraps did you collect?" And they answered, "Seven." Then he said to them, "Do you still not realize?" ' (8:14-21).

This incident immediately follows the feeding of the four thousand. Inexplicably, they have forgotten to take enough bread with them on the boat, even after the previous two occasions that Jesus had to supply bread to the hungry crowds. Many moderns find the miracles of the feeding of the multitude difficult to accept. One would have imagined that such a miracle would have made an impact on the disciples. We would have expected them at this stage to depend on Jesus. When Jesus tells them to beware of the leaven of the Pharisees, they show their incomprehension by saying they have no bread. They are criticized for they, like the Pharisees, have closed and hardened their hearts. (The NJB translation which I quote here refers to a closed mind as explaining the idea of the hardness of heart.) The tables now are turned. The language initially employed to describe outsiders and opponents is now used to depict insiders and friends: seeing, hearing (4:12) and hardness of heart (3:15 cf 6:52, where it is applied to the disciples). All the boundary marks are destroyed. [9]

In 6:37 Jesus charges the disciples with the responsibility of feeding the five thousand. The disciples share the modern person's difficulty in envisaging how to feed so large a group with just two fish and five loaves. They are not in control and they do not reach out in their weakness to be empowered by Jesus to pray and ask for the seemingly impossible. When Jesus does the miraculous they do not understand and come to trust in him. In the next scene the same Jesus comes to the disciples across the water and they find themselves once more full of fear and confusion. Jesus criticizes them for their failure to understand the feeding miracle and for their closed minds (hardness of heart). In 8:2-3 Jesus once again points out the needs of the crowd to the disciples. It is not surprising that the disciples did not know what had to be done in the first feeding, but here, after all they had seen, their lack of understanding is almost beyond belief. This lack of understanding is carried even to the boat scene of 8:14-21.

Mark begins to present the inner group of disciples in contrasting scenes. It is no accident that the final sequence of feeding of the crowd and discussion in the boat is framed by stories of healing of a deaf man and blind man (7:31-37, 8:22-26). These two healing stories have a number of common features and phrases so that the second helps emphasise the first. The healing of blind Bartimaeus is probably a third story in this sequence. Bartimaeus follows Jesus 'on the way' (10:52) as the latter is going to Jerusalem and 'the way' is the way of the cross, a discipleship theme.

'They reached Jericho; and as he left Jericho with his disciples and a great crowd, Bartimaeus - that is, the son of Timaeus - a blind beggar, was sitting at the side of the road. When he heard that it was Jesus of Nazareth, he began to shout and cry out: "Son of David, Jesus, have pity on me." And many of them scolded him and told him to keep quiet, but he only shouted all the louder, "Son of David, have pity on me." Jesus stopped and said, "Call him here." So they called the blind man over. "Courage", they said, "get up: he is calling you." So throwing off his cloak, he jumped up and went to Jesus. Then Jesus spoke. "What do you want me to do for you?" The blind man said to him, "Rabbuni, let me see again." Jesus said to him, "Go; your faith has saved you." And at once his sight returned and he followed him on the way. (10:46-52)

Bartimaeus is one of minor characters that Mark employs in his story.[10] In the face of the incomprehension of the disciples and Peter it is indicated that the road of discipleship is possible. These miracles (7:31-37, 8:22-26, 10:46-52) highlight the deafness and blindness of the disciples by comparison, but the readers are indirectly promised that Jesus is able to create true discipleship in spite of the story of blindness and of denial which we encounter. We are led to ask: what 'way' will he follow? We look to Jesus as the one showing the way and the one who empowers us to follow.

The question of who Jesus is has been raised (4:41; see 6:14-16, and the identification of Jesus by the demons). Perhaps the problem with the disciples is that they fail to recognize correctly who Jesus is. There is ironic distance between the readers and the disciples because Mark has told the reader (1:1) who Jesus is. In 8:27ff the reader discovers that the problem is not resolved when Peter makes a dramatic confession of faith. Peter identifies Jesus as the Christ (8:27). Jesus insists that more must be said about himself:

'Then he began to teach them that the Son of man was destined to suffer grievously, and to be rejected by the Elders and the Chief Priests and the Scribes, and to be put to death, and after three days to rise again; and he said all this quite openly. Then, taking him aside, Peter tried to rebuke him. But turning and seeing his disciples, he rebuked Peter and said to him, "Get behind me, Satan! You are thinking not as God thinks, but as human beings do." ' (8:31-33)

Here we see Peter's failure to understand Jesus. He is called 'Satan' by Jesus. Peter's picture of a glorious Messiah is nipped in the bud. Peter does not understand what Jesus says. After this incident Jesus teaches about discipleship, telling his disciples that following him involves renunciation of self and taking up one's cross and following him (8:34-39). None of us escapes the pain in simply being human, although we do our best to do so. Jesus' recommendation is that, if one is to be a follower, one must face life concretely, one must carry the cross 'on the way' and follow Him to become a new self, transformed in love. The role of a suffering servant (10:45) which Jesus chooses and the meaning of that role for his disciples (following in suffering, becoming servants) challenge and provoke the fear and anxious self-concern portrayed in the disciples. When I found myself facing my own Gethsemane experience this idea of following Jesus hit home. Mark taught me that it was by working through the things that poisoned my life that I would come to a new life. Mark manages to address me in my reality.

In 8:31-10:45 there is clear evidence of careful composition with close attention to the role of the disciples. Three passion announcements (8:31; 9:31; 10:33-34) become the basis of a major three-fold pattern, building up to a climax. Here again we see Mark's predilection for patterns of three. Each of the passion narratives is followed by resistance (8:32-33), or behaviour contrary to that of Jesus (9:33-4, 10:35-41) on the part of the disciples, followed in turn by Jesus' corrective teaching. This teaching points to Jesus' sufferings and the love which he bore them as a model for the disciples (8:33-35). In 10:45 Jesus says: '... the Son of Man himself came not to be served but to serve, and give his life as a ransom for many.' This teaching is often forgotten. It was not just the disciples of Jesus who are uncomprehending before the sayings of Jesus. There were probably more problems in the early church as perceived by Mark: there was the possibility of persecution and martyrdom (8:34-38) and the desire for status and domination (9:33-37; 10:35-45). In 9:33-37 we read:

'They came to Capernaum, and when he got into the house he asked them, "What were you arguing about on the road?" They said nothing, because on the road they had been arguing which of them was the greatest. So he sat down, called the Twelve to him and said, "If anyone wants to be first, he must make himself last of all and servant of all." He then took a little child whom he set among them and embraced, and he said to them, "Anyone who welcomes a little child such as this in my name, welcomes me; and anyone who welcomes me, welcomes not me but the one who sent me." '

The disciples were looking forward to a glorious kingdom where they would be the chosen ones. Now, questioned by Jesus, they fall into silence, not a prayerful silence but one that is born out of embarrassment because of what they were arguing over. Jesus tells them they should have the openness and trust of one of the littler ones, the ones who did not matter in society as it was in Jesus' time. As Chad Myers [11], quoting Alice Miller on the status of children, argues, one should not idealise childhood too much, but see in Jesus' image of the child an oppressed human, without adult rights or privilege; the least of the least. One receives Jesus in receiving the oppressed.

The response of the readers is to disassociate themselves from the egotistical disciples. Jesus had just been speaking about the inevitability of his suffering and dying, yet they are insensitive to him and indulge in crass egotism. [12] Later children would seek to come to Jesus but the disciples tried to usher them away (10:13-16). Jesus was not being heard. He was becoming more isolated from the disciples.

In 10:35-40 we read:

'James and John, the sons of Zebedee, approached him. "Master," they said to him, "we want you to do us a favour." He said to them, "What is it you want me to do for you?" They said to him, "Allow us to sit one at your right hand and the other at your left in your glory." But Jesus said to them, "You do not know what you are asking. Can you drink the cup that I shall drink, or be baptized with the baptism with which I shall be baptized?" They replied, "We can." Jesus said to them, "The cup that I shall drink you shall drink, and with the baptism with which I shall be baptized you shall be baptized, but as for seats at my right hand or my left, these are not mine to grant; they belong to those to whom they have been allotted." '

Each time Jesus tries to get through to his disciples they become even more entrenched in their old way of thinking. The reality of the kingdom is far from them. As Werner Kelber puts it [13], 'with methodical precision the evangelist has each passion-resurrection predication evolve into a clear case of discipleship misconception.' Jesus has been talking about being handed over to Gentiles who would inflict violence on him. James and John, however, ask for places at Jesus' right and left. As we saw it is two thieves who occupy these positions, We can be blinded by our self-interest and not be sensitive to what another is saying or present to them in their hour of need. Mark leads us to question our own attitudes to the people in our lives. At the transfiguration scene where Jesus allowed a glimpse of the glory that would be his after the resurrection, we hear the voice of God telling Peter, James and John to 'listen to him' (9:7). Listening involves putting oneself in the place of another and seeing things through their eyes. The teaching of Jesus not only applies to 'those about him' but involves the reader as well.

These are not the only events (8:31-10:45) that show tension between Jesus and his disciples. In 9:14-29 the disciples fail in an exorcism. The twelve were commissioned

138

to perform exorcisms and up to this they had successfully performed them. In 9:38-40 we hear of the disciples' attempts to end the work of an exorcist who 'was not following us'. The story of the rich young man is followed by a discussion between Jesus and his disciples about riches (10:23-31), which ends with a promise and a warning (10:29-31). The disciples hear of great reward but 'with persecutions'. The reader is being urged to choose between the attitude of Jesus and that of the disciples, but the difficulty of Jesus' demands reminds the readers that in many ways they resemble the disciples. Growth in the way of Christ is a slow process in which one gets to know oneself and comes to know that this journey is not one we undertake on our own. Jesus is with us because he walked the 'way' before us.

Chapter 13 is important for the authors' shaping of the disciples' story. Jesus' discourse has a setting prior to his death and resurrection but deals with events that would come to light after the resurrection. This discourse is placed by Mark before the Passion narrative proper and it helps prepare the readers for Chapters 14-16.

Jesus tells the disciples that they will endure persecutions and must endure to the end (13:9-13). Mark involves the readers directly in 13:14 where the readers suddenly find themselves addressed personally. (He says, 'Let the reader understand',13:14). Any doubts we had that Mark was involving us in his drama are now dispelled. The readers and disciples are warned that they must watch and not be caught asleep (13:37). The disciples would be reminded of this in Gethsemane, as would the readers, but the disciples sleep in their incomprehension. We are being asked for our response.

The importance attached to Judas' betrayal, the flight of the other disciples and Peter's denial appears after Jesus had predicted these events. These predictions serve both to emphasise the events and to lead us to an evaluation of what is happening. The event is then told more than once because our attention is drawn to the events before they happen. This leads us to a negative evaluation of the disciples. This is obvious in the remark about Judas and the use of symbols of close relationship.

'When evening came he arrived with the Twelve. And while they were at table eating, Jesus said, "In truth I tell you, one of you is about to betray me, one of you eating with me." They were distressed and said to him, one after another, "Not me surely?" He said to them, "It is one of the Twelve, one who is dipping into the same dish with me. Yes, the Son of man is going to his fate, as the Scriptures say he will, but alas for that man by whom the Son of man is betrayed! Better for that man if he had never been born." ' (14:17-21)

Judas will later betray Jesus with a kiss (14:44-45): this shows Judas was a loved one and heightens the sense of betrayal. The predication of the scattering of the disciples and the denial by Peter also lead us to a negative view. This is emphasised by the fact that when Jesus tells them they will abandon him they promise just the opposite (14:31). Then the desertion and denial which follows are contrary to what Jesus has taught them in 8:34-37 about following him. The emotions of tragedy are aroused as we witness these events.

All this leads us to appreciate what is happening in the Gethsemane scene (14:32-42). The author emphasizes, through narrating the return of Jesus three times, the failure of the disciples to stay awake and watch. We are prepared for the disciples' lack of sensitivity by Mark's narrative. Now we see first hand the fruits of their incomprehension. We are prepared for their desertion of Jesus in 14:50, in which they all flee. The following flight of the naked young man dramatizes the shamefulness and confusion of the disciples' reaction and satirizes the pretensions of Christians who claim to be ready for martyrdom. The story continues by noting that Peter, who is now the last hope for faithful discipleship among Jesus' close associates, followed Jesus from a distance (14:54). The story of Jesus before the Jewish Council is framed by an introductory reference to Peter's presence (14:54). We see Jesus' fearless disclosure where he answers that he is the Christ, and that they will see the Son of man coming in glory, statements by which he is condemned, (14:62). This contrasts with Peter's denial. The close disciples, the twelve, vanish from the narrative at this point. Yet the readers are led to believe that this is not the end because Jesus promised earlier:

'After the psalms had been sung they left for the Mount of Olives. And Jesus said to them, "You will all fall away, for the scripture says: I shall strike the shepherd and the sheep will be scattered; however, after my resurrection I shall go before you into Galilee." Peter said, "Even if all fall away, I will not." And Jesus said to him, "In truth I tell you, this day, this very night, before the cock crows twice, you will have disowned me three times." But he repeated still more earnestly, "If I have to die with you, I will never disown you." And they all said the same.' (14:26-31)

The promise made by Jesus is repeated by the young man at the empty tomb (16:7); hope is offered us. However in the narrative of Mark, emphasis falls on the disastrous conclusion of the disciples' following of Jesus.

This ending of the disciples' story sends reverberations back through the whole preceding story. The readers might initially have seen in the disciples a reflection of their own faults yet still have hoped for a happy ending to their story. Now they must try to disentangle themselves from what happened. The possibility of following Jesus in our own experience remains open. Following Jesus is the way we come through our Gethsemane experiences.

We are introduced at this point to women disciples of Jesus who stand near Calvary as Jesus dies. Hope seems to be offered here that perhaps there are those in the story who actually follow Jesus with all this involves:

'There were some women watching from a distance. Among them were Mary of Magdala, Mary who was the mother of James the younger and Joset, and Salome. These used to follow him and look after him when he was in Galilee. And many other women were there who had come up to Jerusalem with him.' (15:40-41)

141

They followed Jesus on the way to Jerusalem. On the third day after the crucifixion they come to the empty tomb and are told of Jesus' resurrection and they run away afraid and say nothing to anyone. (16:8) [14] Mark has raised our hopes only to lead us to more disappointment.

It is at this juncture that we appreciate some of the minor characters who people Mark's story. These figures include Bartimaeus, who follows Jesus on the way of the cross (10:52), the anointing woman who intimates the fate of Jesus (14:7-8), Simon of Cyrene who must take up Jesus' cross (15:21), the centurion at the cross who makes the confession of faith which Peter wasn't able to make (15:39) and Joseph of Arimathea, who organises Jesus' burial, as we would have expected those closest to him to do (15:42-47). These are the ones who appear briefly but who replace the disciples in the roles which the disciples closest to Jesus fail to fill. They appear in such brief flashes that they do not allow the readers to shift their attention too much from Jesus and those closest to him. We do not have time to become overly-involved with these characters but they do point to the way which contrasts with the disciples' failure. We are led to examine ourselves as to the way we respond to the good news that is Jesus.

Peter and the Spirituality of Imperfection:

At various stages in our journey we have come across the figure of Peter. In Jesus' wilderness prayer we had the image of Peter interrupting Jesus' silent prayer. Peter and the desciples hunt Jesus down and harass him, reminding him of how much he is in demand as a miracle-worker and a healer.[15]

Peter does not understand Jesus' need for prayer (1:35-39). In 8:27-30 we hear him acclaim Jesus as the Christ but when Jesus tells him of the sufferings that the Son of man must endure, Peter is perturbed and says it must not be so.

He earns a stern rebuke for this from Jesus, who calls him 'Satan' (8:33). At the event of the transfiguration Peter sees but does not understand and doesn't know what to say (9:2-7). In Gethsemane Peter is silent again, but this time because he sleeps while Jesus is in agony. Mark emphasizes in this way Peter's incomprehension. Jesus addresses him as 'Simon', thus indicating that their relationship is strained (14:37). The reader should not be surprised at what happens next. At Jesus' arrest, all the disciples run away but Peter tries to follow Jesus 'from a distance'. But then:

'While Peter was down below in the courtyard, one of the high priest's servant-girls came up. She saw Peter warming himself there, looked closely at him and said, "You too were with Jesus, the man from Nazareth." But he denied it. "I do not know, I do not understand what you are talking about," he said. And he went out into the forecourt, and a cock crowed. The servant-girl saw him and again started telling the bystanders. "This man is one of them." But again he denied it. A little later the bystanders themselves said to Peter, "You are certainly one of them! Why, you are a Galilean." But he started cursing and swearing, "I do not know the man you speak of." And at once the cock crowed for the second time, and Peter recalled what Jesus had said to him, "Before the cock crows twice, you will have disowned me three times." And he burst into tears.' (14:68-72).

Peter, while trying to be committed to Jesus, does not have it within him to break from his fears. He hides from the truth and does not bear witness to Jesus. His boast to Jesus that he would die with him (14:31) is demolished by a servant girl. In shame he is led to tears. He is now ready to follow Jesus back to Galilee.

The picture of Peter seems very negative and indeed it is. The reader is encouraged to learn from Peter, but I would argue that the reader is encouraged also to learn from Jesus' attitude to Peter. As we have seen, Jesus was often exasperated by Peter but all the time it is implied that Jesus still loved Peter, whom he specially chose. Jesus trusted Peter but Peter was not yet worthy of that trust.

In 14:28 Jesus tells the disciples and Peter that he will go before them to Galilee after his resurrection. In 16:7 the young man in the empty tomb tells the woman to tell the disciples, and especially Peter, this. Mark uses his technique of doublets to give this point emphasis. In this way we see Jesus loves Peter and offers him a chance of reconciliation and an opportunity to follow Jesus. He meets Peter at the point of his pain. Peter's wound of betraying Jesus becomes the opportunity for Jesus to meet him again and offer love in reconciliation.

This leads me to consider what may be called a spirituality of imperfection. [16] This is a term I learned from a work by Ernest Kurtz and Katherine Ketcham. It opens with a quotation from Francis T Vincent, the commissioner of baseball. He describes how one learns about failure through playing baseball. I have never played baseball, but I apply his remarks to football. When I was a student we played different groupings in football. One match we played was, to use a euphemism, physically tough. During a lull in proceedings one of the opposition players came over to me and said that it was difficult to believe that two so-called Christian communities could produce a match as rough as this.

We learned a lot about ourselves and our failings in the context of a football match. Albert Camus was once asked where he had gained his knowledge of the psychology of different people. He replied that he had played as goalkeeper for his local team in Algeria and he saw humanity reveal itself in football matches. It takes occasions such as football to remind us that we are fallible human beings.

We are not 'everything' but neither are we 'nothing'. Spirituality is discussed in that space between paradox's extremes, for there we confront our helplessness and powerlessness, our woundedness. In seeking to understand our limitations we seek not only an easing of our pain but an understanding of what it means to hurt and what it means to be healed. [17] Errors are part of our makeup, as football and baseball teach us. Today our error is to deny ourselves, for to be human is to be imperfect, somehow error-prone. To be human is to ask unanswerable questions and to persist in asking them, to be broken and ask for wholeness, to hurt and to try and find a way to healing through the hurt.

This is the forming of Peter. He was not as strong as his boast but his hurt and the hurt he caused became the place where he was accepted by Jesus. [18] The reason we know this is because of the love the early Christian community had for Peter. They saw one empowered by the spirit of Jesus and who looked after his flock, to the point of giving up his life for his people. They could only have known of Peter's early failures because Peter himself made them known. The community knew that Peter's story did not end with the denials but the denials were part of the story of Peter meeting God's love, His forgiveness. Peter would have strengthened those in his community who could have and might, indeed, have failed.

Like 'love', spirituality is a way to 'be'. Following Jesus as fallible followers, we sense our incompleteness, our being somehow unfinished. To be human is to be incomplete, yet yearn for completion; it is to be uncertain, yet long for certainty; to be imperfect, yet crave perfection; to be broken, yet thirst for wholeness. It is as fallible, broken followers that we follow Jesus to come to the presence of God. 'Man is the creature that wants to be God,' Jean-Paul Sartre observed. [19] The spirituality of imperfection wrestles with just that fact. We learn that we are not in control. Imperfection is rather the wound through which we meet God, who accepts us as we are and loves us into life. As Meister Eckhart said: 'To get at the core of God at his greatest, one must first get into the core of himself at his least.' [20] In a modern expression of Eckhart's insight, Jungian analyst Marion Woodman identifies addiction as one of the wounds that lets God in:

'Addiction keeps a person in touch with the God ... At the very point of the vulnerability is where the surrender takes place - that is where the God enters. The God comes through the wound.' [21]

145

We are not the ones in control. God meets us in our wounds and from there we begin afresh.

NOTES ON CHAPTER 6

1. DM Stanley, *Jesus in Gethsemane* (New York: Paulist, 1979), p140
2. DM Stanley, op. cit, p143
3. For this section I am influenced by RC Tannehill, The Disciples in Mark: *The Function of a Narrative Role in the Interpretation of Mark* Edited by WR Telford, (Edinburgh: T&T Clark, 1985), p.169-197 - originally published in JR57 (1977), p386-405. Also I am influenced by RM Fowler, *Let the Reader Understand* (Minneapolis: Fortress Press, 1991) and also R M Fowler, *Reader - Response Critisism: Figuring Mark's Readers* in Mark and Melted, edited by J C Anderson and S D Moore, (Minneapolis: Fortress Press, 1992) p.50-83
4. See Hans Weder, *Disciple, Discipleship* ABDii, p.207-210, also, TP Rausch, *Discipleship in the New Dictionary of Catholic Spirituality*, p.281-284
5. RC Tannehill, see n(3), p175f
6. W Iser, *The Implied Reader: Patterns of Communication in Prose Fiction from Bunyan to Beckett* (Baltimore: John Hopkins University Press, 1974) pxii also p.34, 37, 46, 118-119.
7. W Iser, op. cit, p37
8. RC Tannehill, n(3), p179
9. LE Klosinski, *The Meals in Mark* (Ann Arbor, MI: University Microfilms International, 1988), p.125
10. D Rhoads and D Michie, *Mark a Story: An Introduction to the Narrative of a Gospel* (Philadelphia: Fortress Press, 1982) p131-135
11. C Myers, *Binding the Strong Man: A Political Reading of Mark's Story of Jesus* (Maryknoll, NY: Orbis Books, 1988) p.266-271
12. R.A. Fowler, m(3), p.72
13. W Keller, *Mark's Story of Jesus*: (Philadelphia: Fortress Press, 1979) p.52
14. See ES Malbon, *Fallible Followers: Women and Men in the Gospel of Mark* Semeia (28) 1982, p.29-48

15. ES Malbon, *Narrative Space and Mythic Meaning* (Sheffield; JSOT Press, 1991, p75. She records 'katedioxe' as tracking down Jesus.
16. E Kurtz and K Ketcham, *The Spirituality of Imperfection* (London: Bantam Books, 1994). Also see S Tugwell, *Ways of Imperfection* (London DLT, 1984)
17. E Kurtz and K Ketcham, op. cit, p.2
18. For a summary of Peter in Mark see E Best, *Peter in the Gospel According to Mark*, CBQ40 (1976) p 547-558
19. As quoted by Kurtz and Ketcham, ibid, p.28
20. Ibid, p.28
21. M Woodman, *Worshipping Illusions* Parabola 12:2 (May 1987) p.64

CHAPTER 7

'WHEN IS AN END NOT AN END?'

Mark 16:1-8 is, as we saw, the end of Mark's gospel. In this scene we meet the women who stayed with Jesus at Calvary. Now they come to anoint his body. The account runs as follows:

'When the Sabbath was over, Mary of Magdala, Mary the mother of James, and Salome bought spices with which to go and anoint him. And very early in the morning on the first day of the week they went to the tomb when the sun had risen.

'They had been saying to one another, "Who will roll away the stone for us from the entrance to the tomb?" But when they looked they saw that the stone - which was very big - had already been rolled back. On entering the tomb they saw a young man in a white robe seated on the right-hand side, and they were struck with amazement. But he said to them, "There is no need to be so amazed. You are looking for Jesus of Nazareth, who was crucified: he has risen, he is not here. See, here is the place where they laid him. But you must go and tell his disciples and Peter: He is going ahead of you to Galilee; that is where you will see him, just as he told you." And the women came out and ran away from the tomb because they were frightened out of their wits; and they said nothing to anyone, for they were afraid.'(16:1-8)

In the main narrative of his gospel, events run headlong into another. He uses the simple connections 'and' (*Kai*) to breathlessly go from one incident to the next. Here things appear more gently, on the surface at least.

The women come to the tomb wondering who will roll away the stone, but instead they find the stone rolled away and a young man sitting there clothed in a white robe. The appearance of this young man and, indeed, his very clothing stand in stark contrast to the young man who ran away naked after Jesus had been taken prisoner. (14:51f). Here all is calm. The young man tells the women not to be afraid because Jesus is risen. This simple statement shows us that the cross was not the end, but God had vindicated Jesus by raising him from death. It is from this perspective that Mark contemplated the career and teaching of Jesus.

He then goes on to tell the women that Jesus had gone on ahead of them to Galilee where they will see him. They are told to tell this to the disciples and especially to Peter. The pain of the disciples and Peter must have been intolerable. They experienced grief when they lost Jesus, shame when they ran away and confusion because they had not understood Jesus. Their feelings resonate with many of our negative experiences. Kris Kristofferson speaks in one of his songs of failure locking him out on the wrong side of the door and 'lonesome being more than a state of mind'. [1] He encapsulates in these words the feelings I have experienced. Fear, lonesomeness, depression and shame can lock us into ourselves. Yet the failed disciples are told that Jesus will meet them again. Reconciliation is extended to them and the chance of a new beginning is proffered. They don't have to stay in their despair. Jesus meets them there and leads them to new life.

This would appear to be an ideal place to finish the gospel. It would not be Mark, however, if he allowed things to remain as they are. He finishes the gospel with a jolt. He tells us that the women said nothing to anyone because they were afraid. (16:8) [2]

What on earth is happening here? The reader remembers that Mark wrote from a post-resurrection perspective and the message of reconciliation did get through to the disciples and Peter. If this were not so then we not have had a gospel. This does not let us off the hook though.

I was looking for words to help us understand what Mark is doing. I got an interesting insight from a friend whom I told about the ending. She said of the ending, 'How vulnerable!' This opened up insights for me into Mark, his gospel and its ending.

Vulnerable is a good word to help us understand the Jesus of Mark. Mark doesn't have the lofty statements of John, who told us God is love (1 Jn 4:8, 16); yet even though Mark doesn't explicitly state this, nevertheless in his gospel love sums up the spirit and motivating force in Jesus' preaching and healings. The words of the monk Zossima in Dostoyevsky's novel, *The Brothers Karamazov*, are apposite here:

' ... love in action is a harsh and dreadful thing compared with love in dreams. Love in dreams is greedy for immediate action, rapidly performed and in the sight of all. Men will even give their lives if only the ordeal does not last long but is soon over, with all looking on and applauding as though on the stage. But active love is labour and fortitude, and for some people too perhaps a complete science. But I predict that just when you see with horror that in spite of all your efforts you are getting further from your goal, instead of nearer to it - at that very moment I predict that you will reach it and behold clearly the miraculous power of the Lord who has been all the time loving and mysteriously guiding you.' [3]

Jesus is the living embodiment of this love in the gospel of Mark. In 16:1-8 the young man tells of Jesus offering reconciliation to the failed disciples. In the main narrative section we see the healings of Jesus because of his compassion for those wounded by life (e.g. 5:1-20 - the healing of the Gadarene demoniac). His love was defenceless. He could offer no resistance to those who would feel threatened by his ministry and who would condemn him to an ignominious death. This vulnerability of Jesus is further highlighted by Mark's ending.

16:8 has the effect of jolting the readers away from the world of Mark to the reality of their ordinary lives. However, after reading or hearing the gospel of Mark the readers are not the same. Here they have met Jesus and are asked for a response in their daily living. The readers are the conclusion of Mark. We have been introduced to failed disciples and a rejected Jesus. Yet Jesus is the son of God and reveals compassion to those who enter his world. He is the one who meets people in their pain. If we have met Jesus through the hands of Mark, then we do not remain unchanged. How we respond in faith to Jesus determines our spirituality. In short, my response to Jesus is the end of Mark's gospel. I am my own conclusion to the experience of reading Mark. I have seen how others fail to understand Jesus and I am being asked how I hear Jesus and what my response to him is. I have to meet him in my pain. The rest of my life is a working out of this relationship - the true end of Mark's gospel.

NOTES ON CHAPTER 7

1. K Kristofferson, 'To Beat the Devil' from the album 'Me and Bobby McGee' (Monument records, 1973).
2. For discussion of 16:8 as the ending of Mark see R Meye, *Mark 16:18 - 'The Ending of Mark's Gospel'*, Biblical Research 14 (1969), p.33-44; J Peterson, *When is an End not an End? Literary Reflections on the Ending of Mark's Narrative*, Interpretation 34 (1980), p.151-166. W Harrington, *Mark: Realistic Theologian* (Dublin: Columbia Press, 1996), p17, and 29.
3. F Dostoyevsky, *The Brothers Karamazov*, bk 2 Chapter 4

ABBREVIATIONS

Old Testament

Genesis	Gn	Proverbs	Prv
Exodus	Ex	Qoheleth	Qo
Leviticus	Lv	Song of Songs	Sq
Numbers	Nm	Wisdom	Wis
Deuteronomy	Dt	Sirach	Sir
Joshua	Jos	Isaiah	Is
Judges	Jgs	Jeremiah	Jer
Ruth	Ru	Lamentations	Lam
1 Samuel	1 Sm	Baruch	Bar
2 Samuel	2 Sm	Ezekiel	Ez
1 Kings	1 Kgs	Daniel	Dn
2 Kings	2 Kgs	Hosea	Hos
1 Chronicles	1 Chr	Joel	Jl
2 Chronicles	2 Chr	Amos	Am
Ezra	Ezr	Obadiah	Ob
Nehemiah	Heh	Jonah	Jon
Tobit	Tb	Micha	Mi
Judith	Jdt	Nahum	Na
Esther	Est	Habakkuk	Hb
1 Maccabees	1 Mc	Zephaniah	Zep
2 Maccabees	2 Mc	Haggai	Hg
Job	Jb	Zechariah	Zec
Psalms	Ps(s)	Malachi	Mal

New Testament

Matthew	Mt	1 Corinthians	1 Cor
Mark	Mk	2 Corinthians	2 Cor
Luke	Lk	Galatians	Gal
John	Jn	Ephesians	Eph
Acts of the Apostles	Acts	Philippians	Phil

Romans	Rom	Colossians	Col
1 Thessalonians	1 Thes	1 Peter	1 Pt
2 Thessalonians	2 Thes	2 Peter	2 Pt
1 Timothy	1 Tim	1 John	1 Jn
2 Timothy	2 Tim	2 John	2 Jn
Titus	Ti	3 John	3 Jn
Philemon	Phlm	Jude	Jude
Hebrews	Heb	Relelation	Rev
James	Jas		

Other Abbreviations:

ABD:	Anchor Bible Dictionary
BiB:	Biblica
EH:	Historica Ecclesiastica
CBQ:	Catholic Biblical Quarterly
Int:	Interpretation
JR:	Journal of Religion
NJBC:	New Jerome Biblical Commentary
NTS:	New Testament Studies
IQH:	Thanksgiving Hymn for Quamran
IQM:	War Scroll from Quamran
RB:	Revue Biblique
TDNT:	Theological Word - Dictionary of the New Testament
ZNW:	Zeitschrift für die neu testamentliche Wissenschaft

.